Nursery Needlepoint

Nursery Needlepoint

FIONA McTAGUE

30 delightful needlework projects

Ebury Press London

To Dave, Lucy and Molly
for all their love, support and inspiration

Contents

Introduction

The enchanting world of nursery rhymes and childhood folklore has captured my imagination ever since I was a child. And now, with little ones of my own (Lucy and Molly), my fascination with the magic of childhood has been re-kindled providing me with the inspiration to create *Nursery Needlepoint*.

In this book, you'll discover a wide range of needlepoint and cross-stitch designs that I'm sure you will will love to make. Some are simple – such as the Ring-a-ring o' roses table mat and the Nursery numbers sampler – and others are more intricate – such as the Wee Willie Winkie pyjamas bag and She sells sea shells duffle bag – yet all come complete with easy-to-follow instructions and detailed design charts. Whether it's the Noah's ark rug, the Count to ten book or the Humpty Dumpty footstool which you choose to make, I hope the beautiful designs will enhance your child's room and, in time, become treasured heirlooms for future generations of your family.

Nursery Rhymes Birth Sampler

Here are images taken from nursery rhymes
which, when combined with birth details,
make a charming sampler that will be a special
memento for both child and parents.

Full making instructions are given on page 45.

Nursery Alphabet

This delightful nursery
alphabet includes a picture for every letter
from A to Z: apple to zebra.

Full making instructions are given on page 49.

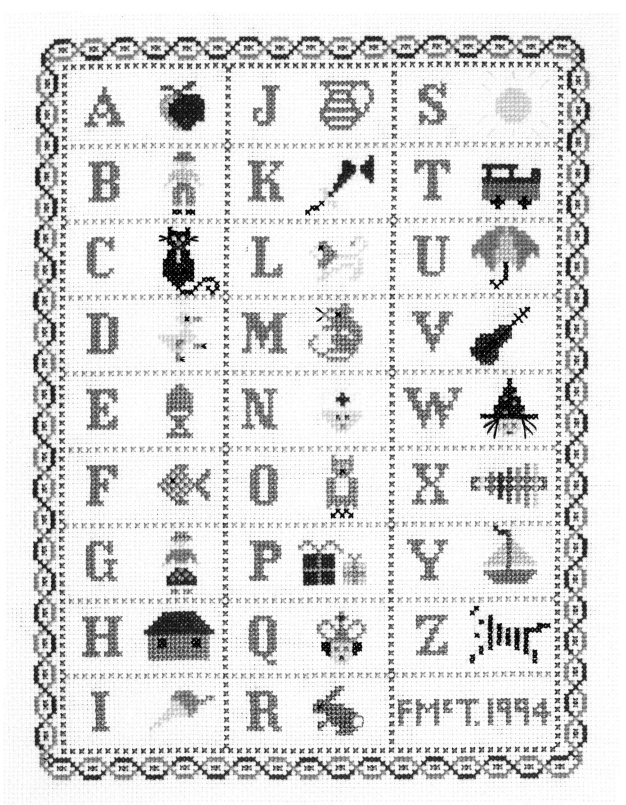

Rock-A-Bye Baby

Rock-a-bye baby on the tree top.
When the wind blows, your cradle with rock,
When the bough breaks, your cradle will fall.
And down will come baby, cradle, and all.

Full making instructions are given on page 47.

Girls and Boys

Girls and boys come out to play
The moon doth shine as bright as day;
Leave your supper and leave your sleep,
And come to your playfellows in the street.

Full making instructions are given on page 46.

Five Little Ducks

Five little ducks went swimming one day,
Over the hills and far away.

Full making instructions are given on page 52.

Higgledy, Piggledy, My Fat Hen

Higgledy, piggledy, my fat hen,
She lays eggs for gentlemen.
Gentlemen come every day
To see what my fat hen can lay.

Full making instructions are given on page 51.

The Queen of Hearts

The Queen of Hearts, she made some tarts.
All on a summer's day.

Full making instructions are given on page 53.

Wee Willie Winkie

Wee Willie Winkie runs through the town,
Upstairs and downstairs in his night-gown.

Full making instructions are given on page 55.

Ride a Cock-Horse

Ride a cock-horse to Banbury Cross,
To see a fine lady upon a white horse.

Full making instructions are given on page 59.

Lavender's Blue

Lavender's blue, dilly dilly, lavender's green,
When I am King, dilly dilly, you shall be Queen.

Full making instructions are given on page 60.

I Have Built a Little House

I have built a little house, With a chimney tall;
A roof of red, A garden shed, And a garden wall.

Full making instructions are given on page 62.

Jingle Bells

Jingle bells, jingle bells, jingle all the way.
Oh what fun it is to ride in a one horse open sleigh.

Full making instructions are given on page 65.

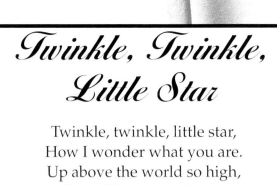

Twinkle, Twinkle, Little Star

Twinkle, twinkle, little star,
How I wonder what you are.
Up above the world so high,
Like a diàmond in the sky,
Twinkle, twinkle, little star,
How I wonder what you are.

Full making instructions are given on page 67.

This Little Piggy
Went To Market

... and this little piggy went
wee wee wee, all the way home.

Full making instructions are given on page 77.

She Sells Sea Shells

She sells sea shells on the sea shore.

Full making instructions are given on page 79.

Nursery Numbers

This charming sampler took its inspiration
from a number of different rhymes and the
combination of motifs and numbers makes a useful
and fun counting chart.

Full making instructions are given on page 81.

See-Saw, Margery Daw

See-saw, Margery Daw,
Johnny shall have a new master;
He shall have but a penny a day,
Because he can't go any faster.

Full making instructions are given on page 83.

Sleep, Baby, Sleep

Sleep, baby, sleep,
Our cottage vale is deep.

Full making instructions are given on page 85.

The Cow Jumped Over the Moon

Hey, diddle diddle, the cat and the fiddle,
The cow jumped over the moon.

Full making instructions are given on page 93.

Traditional Sampler

A timeless sampler, decorated with
traditional lettering and motifs, that will enhance
any child's room.

Full making instructions are given on page 95.

Punch and Judy

This is a really special door placard decorated
with a pugnacious Punch and poor old Judy,
together with the child's name.

Full making instructions are given on page 97.

Count to Ten

An entertaining cloth book which uses colourful
everyday objects to count from one to ten.

Full making instructions are given on page 99.

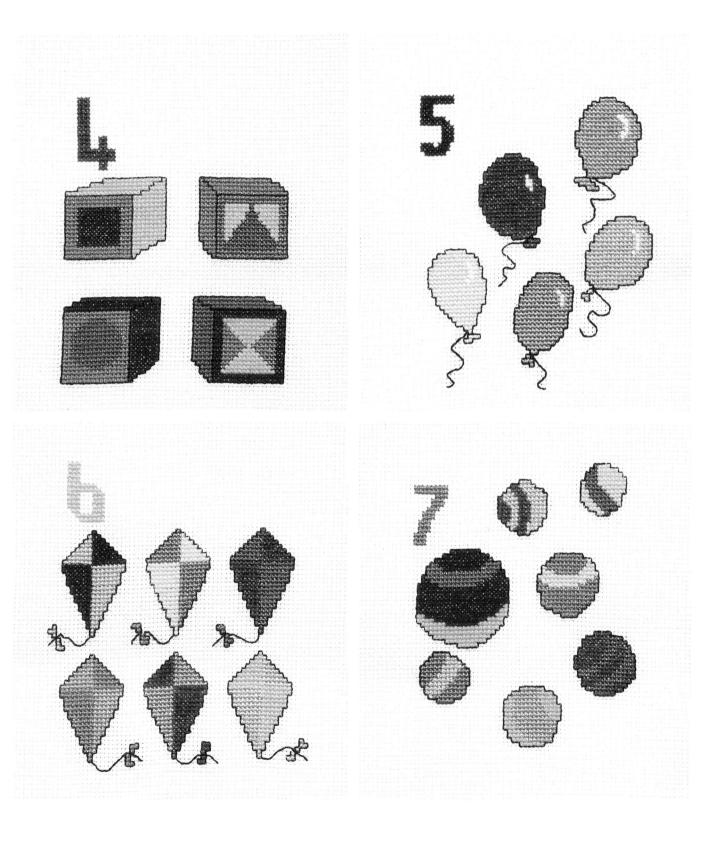

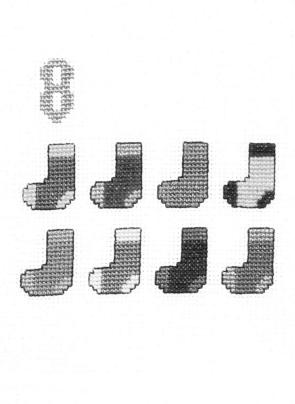

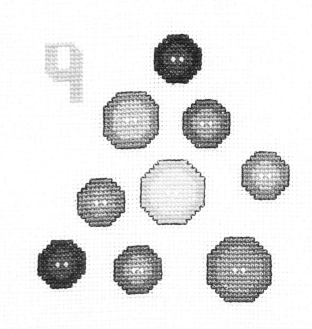

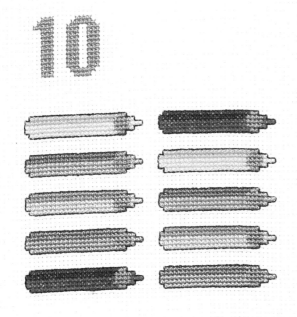

Noah's Ark

A chunky rug showing the animals going two by
two into Noah's Ark, this is an enchanting way to
tell a story that always delights the imagination.

Full making instructions are given on page 111.

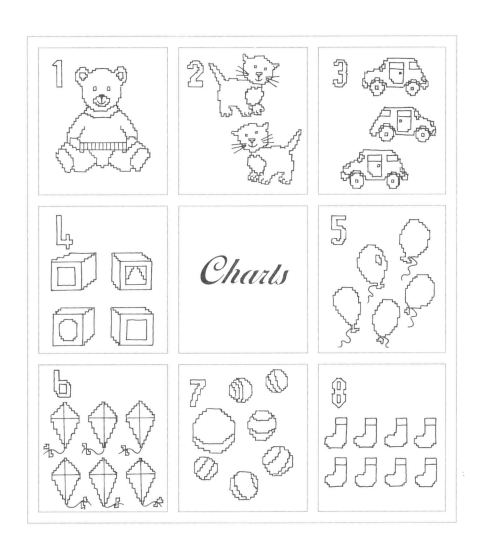

Charts

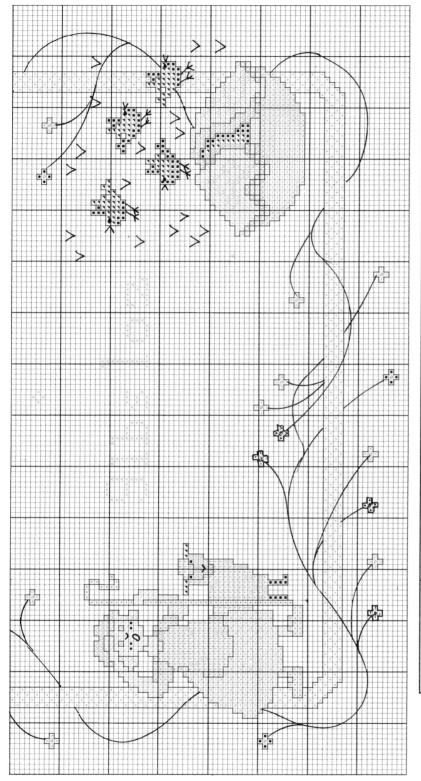

Nursery Rhymes

Illustrated on page 11

DESIGN SIZE
27 x 39cm (10½ x 15½in)

MATERIALS
Madeira 6-strand cotton embroidery thread, 10m (11yd) spiral packs:
2 x 1810 dark grey
1 x white; 0108 yellow; 0210 red; 0213 light red; 0404 pink; 0909 light blue; 0911 mid-blue; 1211 light green; 1213 green; 1801 mid-grey; 1803 light grey; 2009 brown; 2011 dark tan; 2013 light tan; 2309 peach; black
31 x 44cm (12½ x 17½in) piece of DMC 14-count, off-white Aida fabric

TO STITCH
The original design was worked in cross stitch and finished with backstitch and french knots. Use three strands of the thread for the cross stitches and two strands for embroidery. Position the design so that its centre is at the centre of the Aida fabric.

For letters for the child's name, see the alphabet charts on page 114. For the numerals for the date of birth, see the chart on page 115. Work out the arrangements of the letters and numbers on graph paper before stitching.

KEY
T white		1213 green	
0108 yellow		1801 mid-grey	
0210 red		1803 light grey	
0213 light red		1810 dark grey	
0404 pink		2009 brown	
0909 light blue		2011 dark tan	
0911 mid-blue		2013 light tan	
1211 light green		2309 peach	

EMBROIDERY
0108   yellow backstitch for birds' legs, feet and beaks
1801   mid-grey backstitch for border
1810   dark grey backstitch for all motifs
black   backstitch for birds' outlines and small blackbirds
black   french knots for birds' eyes

Girls and Boys Come Out To Play

Illustrated on page 13

MATERIALS

Madeira 6-strand cotton embroidery thread, 10m (11yd) spiral packs:
1 x 0113 dark yellow; 0212 red; 1107 kingfisher; 1207 green; 2012 light coffee; 2211 gold; black
52 x 9cm (21 x 3½in) piece of DMC 11-count, white Aida fabric
50cm (20in) wide white towel

TO STITCH

The original design was worked in cross stitch and finished with backstitch. Use three strands of the thread for the cross stitches and two strands for the embroidery. Position the design so that its centre is at the centre of the Aida fabric.

KEY

+	0113 dark yellow	∘	2012 light coffee
✕	0212 red	⊿	2211 gold
−	1107 kingfisher	■	black
⊚	1207 green		

EMBROIDERY

black backstitch for all outlines
black french knot for the ducks' eyes

TO MAKE THE TOWEL BORDER

1 Turn under the ends of the border by 1cm (½in) and pin and baste the border across one end of the towel.
2 To attach the strip securely to the towel, use satin stitch and machine along the raw edges of the border, covering them completely with the width of the satin stitch. Slip stitch the turned allowance to the towel sides to finish.

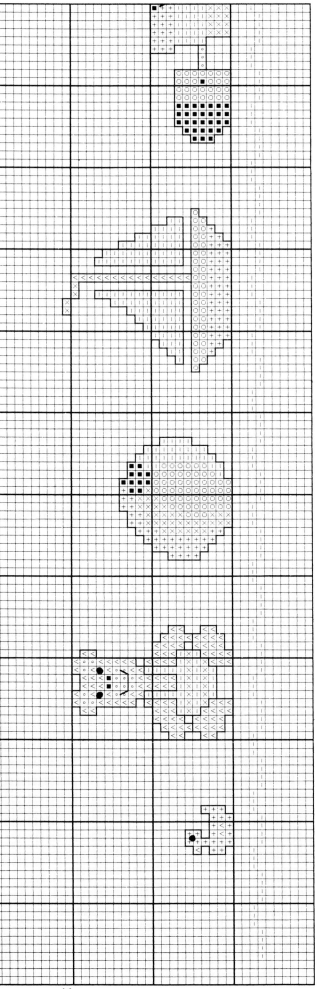

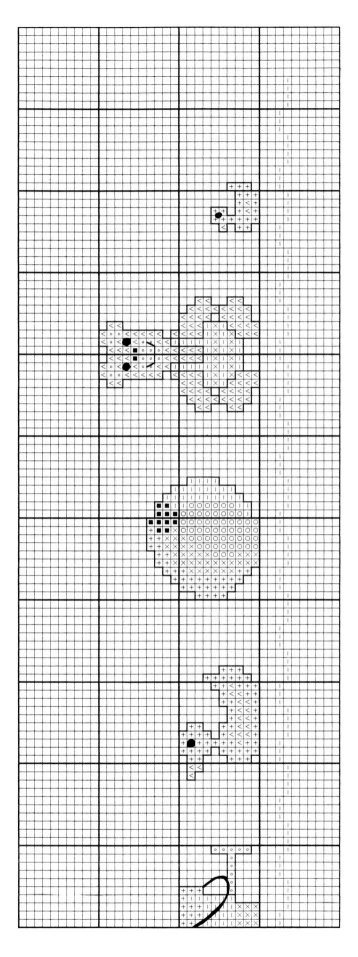

Rock-A-Bye Baby

Illustrated on page 13

MATERIALS
Madeira 6-strand cotton embroidery
thread, 10m (11yd) spiral packs:
1 x 0110 yellow; 0404 pale pink; 0405 mid-
pink; 0412 dark pink; 1211 light green;
1213 dark green; 1711 mid-blue
8 x 7cm (3½ x 3in) piece of DMC 14-count
waste canvas
Baby's towel with hood

TO STITCH
The original design was worked in cross
stitch. Use three strands of the thread
throughout. The motif was centred on
the hood, but you may decide to position
the motif elsewhere. For the baby's initial,
see the alphabet chart on page 116.

This design is worked using waste fabric
to act as a stitch guide. The waste fabric
is tacked in place wherever you choose
your design to appear, the motif is
stitched, and then the waste fabric is
carefully removed.

Cut a piece of waste canvas to measure
8 x 7cm (3½ x 3in), tack in place on the
towel, and stitch the motif through both
layers. Once the cross stitch is complete,
begin cutting away the excess waste
canvas around the stitched motif. Leave
the thread ends which run behind the
cross stitch long enough to pull out.
Gently pull out each of these threads,
one by one.

KEY

⬚	0110	yellow	╱	1211 light green
−	0404	pale pink	✕	1213 dark green
I	0405	mid-pink	•	1711 mid-blue
+	0412	dark pink		

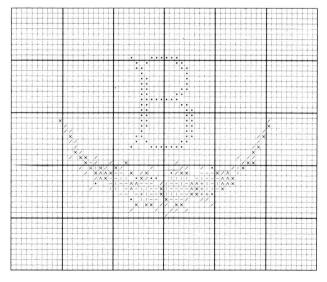

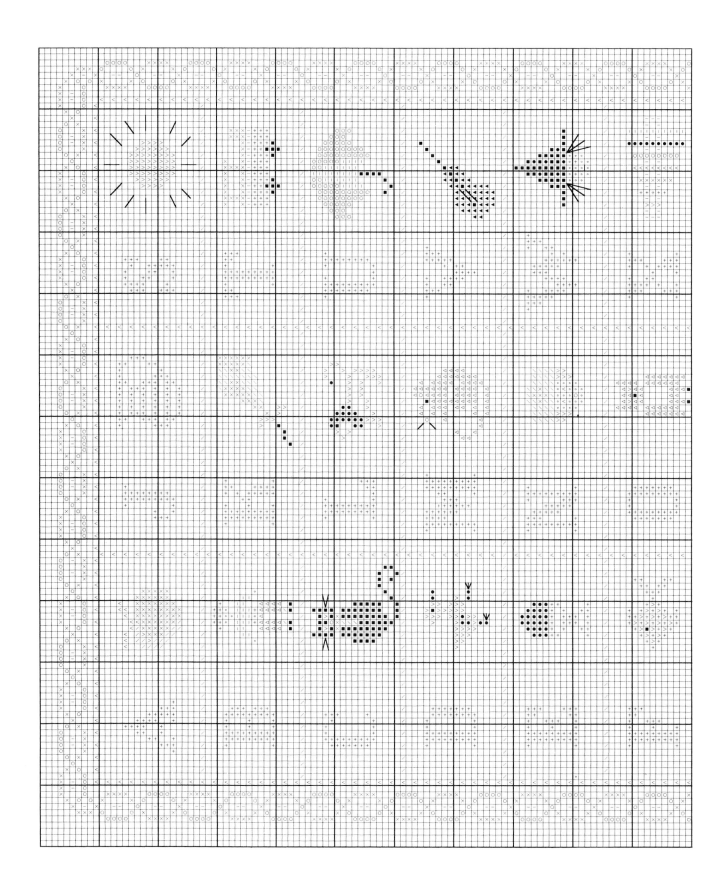

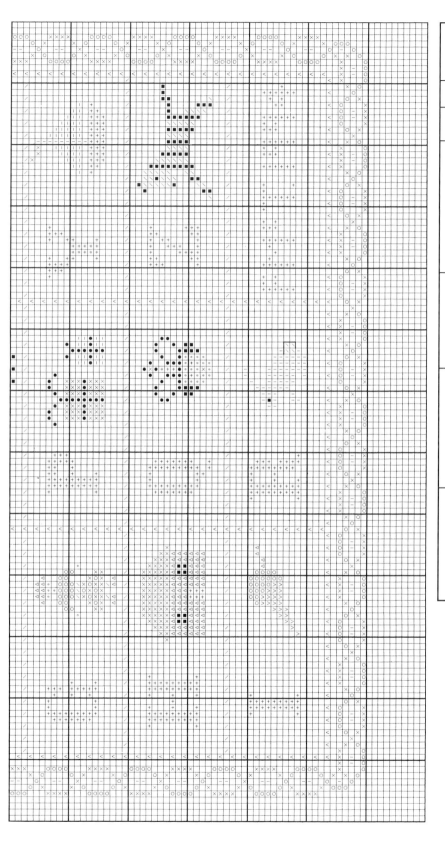

Nursery Alphabet

Illustrated on page 12

DESIGN SIZE
22 x 30cm (8¾ x 12in)

MATERIALS
Madeira 6-strand cotton embroidery thread, 10m (11yd) spiral packs:
1 x white; 0109 yellow; 0210 red; 0305 peach; 0414 pink; 0911 blue; 1002 pale blue; 1401 light green; 1403 dark green; 1801 grey; 1911 mink; 2212 gold; 2305 copper brown; black
27 x 35cm (11 x 14in) piece of DMC 14-count, ivory Aida fabric

TO STITCH
The original design was worked in cross stitch and finished with backstitch. Use three strands of the thread for the cross stitches and two strands for embroidery. Position the design so that its centre is at the centre of the Aida fabric.

KEY

☑	white	◥ 1401	light green
☑ 0109	yellow	◣ 1403	dark green
☒ 0210	red	▯ 1801	grey
○ 0305	peach	△ 1911	mink
◎ 0414	pink	● 2212	gold
✚ 0911	blue	▲ 2305	copper
▬ 1002	pale blue		brown
		■ black	

EMBROIDERY
0109 yellow backstitch for sun and owl's eyes
0210 red backstitch for witch's mouth
1801 grey backstitch for rabbit's tail
black backstitch for cat and mouse whiskers, duck's feet, violin strings and witch's hair

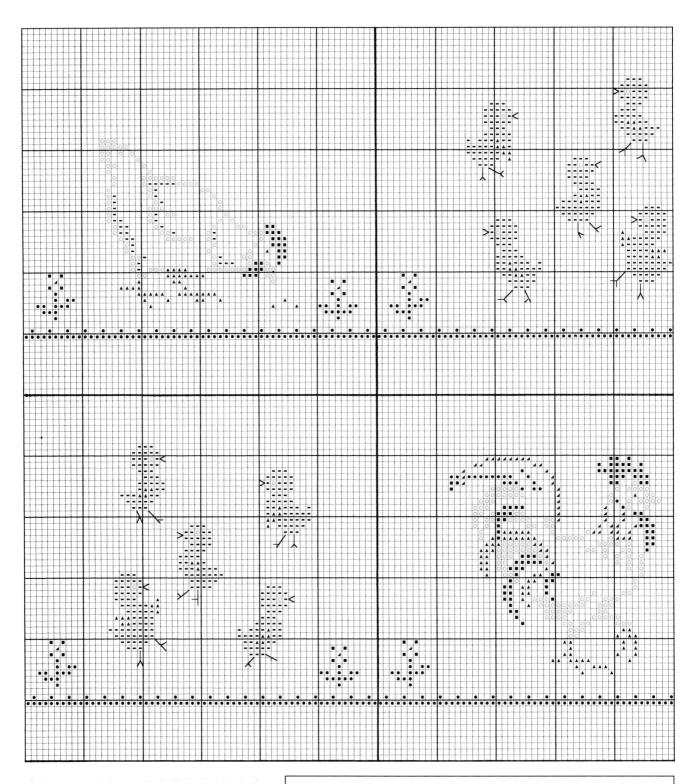

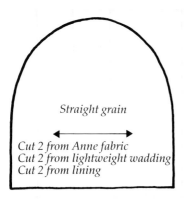

Straight grain

Cut 2 from Anne fabric
Cut 2 from lightweight wadding
Cut 2 from lining

Add 1cm (½in) seam allowances

TO MAKE THE EGG COSIES

1 Cut out strips of gingham on the bias which are 10cm (4in) wide and long enough to fit around the edge of the cosy. Fold the strips in half lengthways with a 1cm (½in) turning on each side.
2 Using the template, cut two pieces of wadding and two pieces of lining per cosy.
3 For each half of each cosy, lay the embroidered piece up, lay a piece of wadding over the embroidery and a piece of lining, face down, on top of the whole. Pin and baste the bottom edge of the three layers together. Then machine stitch leaving a 1cm (½in) seam allowance. Turn right sides out. Press.
4 Pin and baste together both halves of each cosy, right sides out, leaving the bottom edge open. Stitch together leaving a 1cm (½in) seam allowance.
5 Place the gingham edging over the seam covering the front and back and attach using zigzag stitch. Hand stitch the edges to finish off.

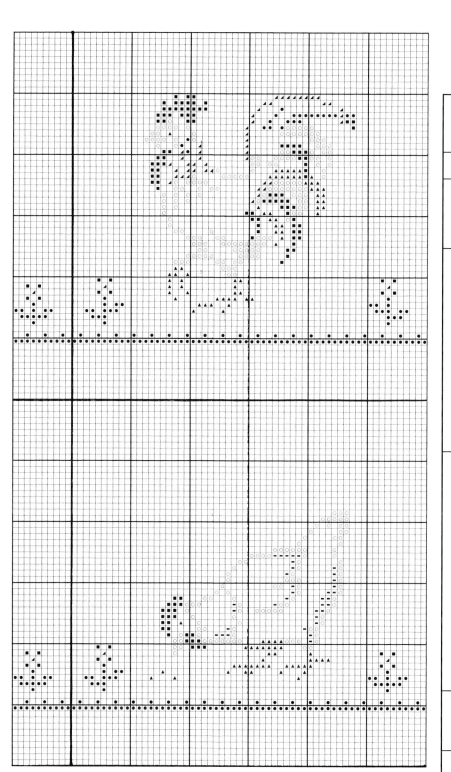

Higgledy, Piggledy, My Fat Hen

Illustrated on page 14

DESIGN SIZE
The completed table mat measures
50 x 35cm (20 x 14in)
Each egg cosy measures
12 x 12cm (4¾ x 4¾in)

MATERIALS
Madeira 6-strand cotton embroidery
thread, 10m (11yd) spiral packs:
1 x 0113 yellow; 0212 red; 0311 orange;
1108 kingfisher; 1408 green; 2211 gold
For table mat:
55 x 40cm (22 x 16in) piece of DMC 18-
count, white Anne fabric
For each egg cosy:
Two 14 x 14cm (5¾ x 5¾in) pieces of DMC
18-count, white Anne fabric
Two 14 x 14cm (5¾ x 5¾in) pieces of
lightweight wadding
Two 14 x 14cm (5¾ x 5¾in) pieces of
white lightweight polyester cotton lining
1m x 27cm (1yd x 10½in) gingham cotton

TO STITCH
The original design was worked in cross
stitch. Use two strands of the thread
throughout.

Before beginning to stitch the table mat,
baste central positioning lines for each
motif in each square following the chart.
Remove the basting stitches when you
have finished the embroidery.

Before beginning to stitch the egg cosies,
first draw the egg cosy template (opposite)
to its correct size (1 square = 2.5cm [1in])
on a piece of card. Cut out the template,
position on the Aida fabric on the
straight grain, draw around it and cut out
two pieces for each cosy. Stitch any one
of the motifs from the chart in the centre
of the front piece of fabric.

KEY

⊟ 0113 yellow		◪ 1108 kingfisher
■ 0212 red		● 1408 green
⊙ 0311 orange		▲ 2211 gold

TO MAKE THE TABLE MAT
1 When the embroidery is complete,
trim it very carefully to the finished size
of 50 x 35cm (20 x 14in).
2 To make a fringe, work a single row of
hem stitching, taking two threads for
each stitch, 2cm (¾in) in from the edge.
Then pull out the threads up to this line.

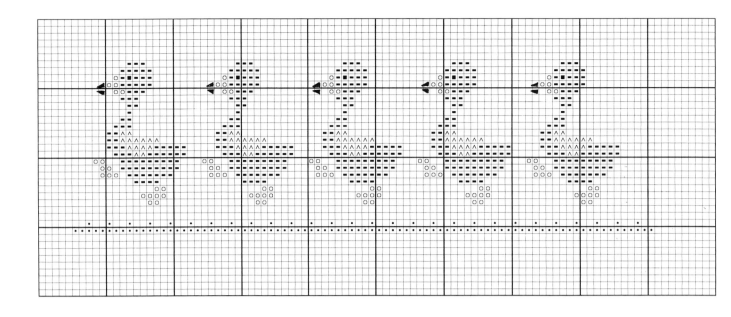

Five Little Ducks

Illustrated on page 14

DESIGN SIZE
The completed bib measures
35 x 24cm (14 x 9½in)

MATERIALS
Madeira 6-strand cotton embroidery
thread, 10m (11yd) spiral packs:
1 x 0113 yellow; 0311 orange; 1408 green;
2211 gold; black
Two 33 x 28cm (13 x 11in) pieces of DMC
11-count, off-white Aida fabric
1m (1yd) gingham cotton
Small piece of velcro

TO STITCH
The original design was worked in cross
stitch. Use three strands of the thread
throughout.

Before beginning to stitch, first draw the
bib template (right) to its correct size
(1 square = 2.5cm [1in]) on a piece of
card. Cut out the template, position on
the Aida fabric on the straight grain,
draw around it and cut out two pieces.

Taking one of the pieces of fabric, arrange
the ducks so that they are centred to its
width and the bottom of the motif is
2.5cm (1in) above the bottom of the bib.

KEY

⊟	0113 yellow	◮	2211 gold
⊙	0311 orange	■	black
⊡	1408 green	⊡	0311 orange, half cross stitch

TO MAKE THE BIB
1 Cut two strips of gingham on the bias
which are 1.5cm (¾in) wide and are long
enough to fit around the outside and
inside edges of the bib.
2 Pin and baste the bib front and back
together with the wrong sides facing
each other and the gingham edging
between, leaving 5mm (¼in) protruding.
Zigzag stitch the three layers together.
Sew on the velcro at the neck.

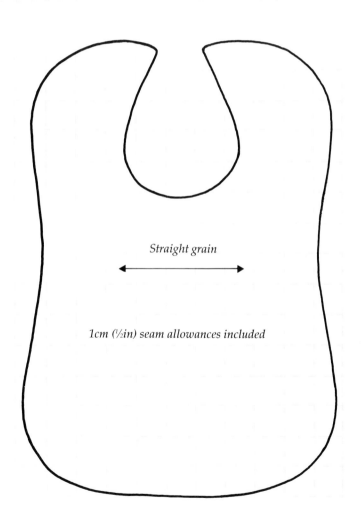

Straight grain

1cm (½in) seam allowances included

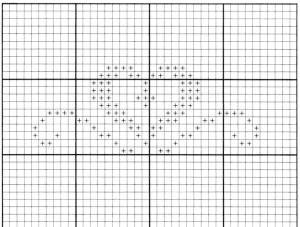

The Queen of Hearts

Illustrated on page 16

DESIGN SIZE
The completed pinny measures
70 x 29cm (28 x 11½in)

MATERIALS
Madeira 6-strand cotton embroidery thread, 10m (11yd) spiral packs:
1 x white; ecru; 0109 yellow; 0211 red; 0305 flesh; 0405 pink; 1710 light blue; 1711 blue; 1713 charcoal; 2011 coffee; 2212 gold
71 x 137cm (28 x 54in) DMC 25-count, Dublin linen

TO STITCH
The original design was worked in cross stitch and finished with backstitch. Use three strands of the thread for the cross stitches and two strands for embroidery.

Before beginning to stitch, cut the following pieces from the linen:
76 x 30cm (30 x 12in) piece for the apron
15 x 14cm (6 x 5½in) piece for the pocket
Two 46 x 7.5cm (18 x 3in) pieces for ties
30 x 7.5cm (12 x 3in) piece for waistband

The heart motifs are positioned just above the apron's hem. Centre one motif to the width of the fabric and leave a space of 8 stitches between each heart. Continue around the hem until the hearts reach the side edges, keeping the side motifs complete. Stitch the Queen of Hearts figure in the centre of the pocket.

KEY
⊡	white	⊼	0405 pink
⊘	ecru	·	1710 light blue
○	0109 yellow	×	1711 blue
+	0211 red	⊠	2011 coffee
⊻	0305 flesh	⊟	2212 gold

EMBROIDERY
1713 charcoal backstitch for all outlines

TO MAKE THE PINNY
1 On the pocket, turn a 1cm (½in) hem to the wrong side along the top edge and slipstitch in place. Turn under 1cm (½in) along each of the three sides of the pocket and slipstitch the whole pocket to the pinny, 7.5cm (3in) up from the bottom and in from the right-hand edge.
2 Gather the top of the pinny by sewing two rows of running stiches 5mm (¼in) and 1cm (½in) in from the edge. Pull both the loose ends and evenly gather to fit the 30cm (12in) long waistband.
3 With the right side of the waistband to the right side of the pinny, pin and baste the waistband in place. Machine stitch 1cm (½in) in from the edge. Remove the basting and running stitches. Turn under 1cm (½in) along the edge, fold the waistband in half and slipstitch in place on the wrong side along the line of machine stitching.
4 On each tie, turn a 1cm (½in) hem to the wrong side along the two long edges and one of the short edges. Mitre the corners and slipstitch the hem in place.
5 To attach the ties, make a pleat in the unhemmed end of each tie, insert them into the folded edges of the waistband, turning in the extra 1cm (½in), and slipstitch in position.

↑ *Chart continued on pages 56-7*

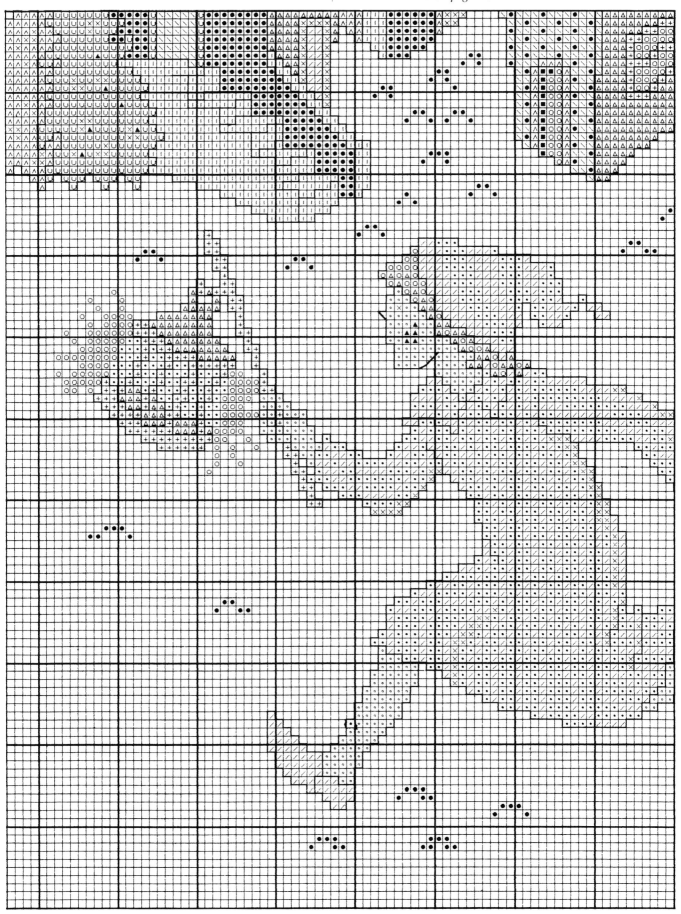

Chart continued on pages 56-7 ↑

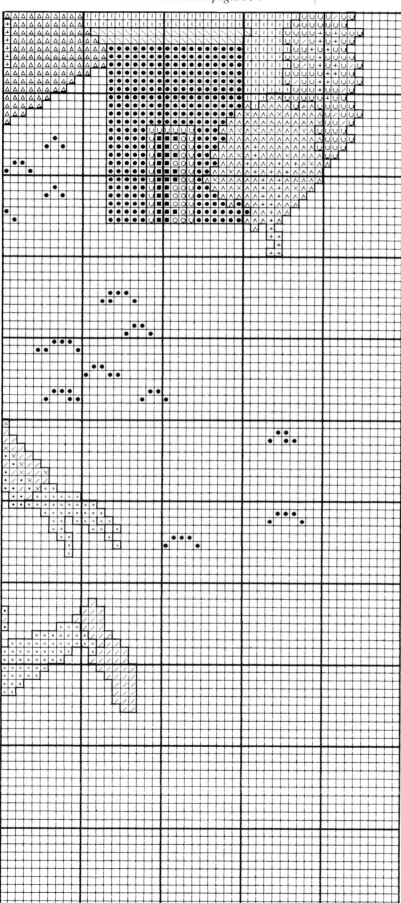

Wee Willie Winkie

Illustrated on page 17

DESIGN SIZE
The completed bag measures
50 x 24cm (20 x 9½in)

MATERIALS
Madeira 6-strand cotton embroidery thread, 10m (11yd) spiral packs:
2 x 1911 beige; 2011 coffee
1 x white; 0110 yellow; 0405 pink; 0810 plum; 1107 kingfisher; 1406 pine green; 1503 moss green; 1707 slate blue; 1810 charcoal; 2001 light beige; 2009 brown; 2309 flesh
52 x 26cm (21 x 10½in) piece of 14-count, pale blue Aida fabric
52 x 26cm (21 x 10½in) piece of pale blue lining cotton
140cm (55in) cord for drawstring

TO STITCH
The original design was worked in cross stitch and finished with backstitch. Use three strands of the thread for the cross stitches and two strands for embroidery. Position the design so that its foot is at the bottom of the Aida fabric.

KEY

·	white	✕	1707 slate blue
○	0110 yellow	■	1810 charcoal
▲	0405 pink	●	1911 beige
◲	0810 plum	⊺	2001 light beige
◿	1107 kingfisher	+	2009 brown
∧	1406 pine green	△	2011 coffee
∪	1503 moss green	○	2309 flesh

EMBROIDERY
☐ 1810 charcoal backstitch for all outlines

TO MAKE THE PYJAMA BAG
1 For the lining, with right sides of back and front facing, join the side and base seams with a 1cm (½in) seam allowance. Trim the seam allowances and corners.
2 Make the bag in the same way, but turn to right side after trimming.
3 With right sides facing, join lining to outside of bag at top and stitch together. Turn right sides out.
4 On the front of the bag make two 1cm (½in) wide eyelet holes through both the bag and the lining. They should be positioned 3cm (1¼in) in from the side seams and 7.5cm (3in) down from the top of the bag. Repeat on the back.
5 To make a drawstring panel, machine stitch twice right around the bag, once 1cm (½in) above the eyelet holes and again 1cm (½in) below the eyelet holes. Insert the drawstring cord through the drawstring panel using the eyelets. Secure the cord.

Lavender's Blue

Illustrated on page 19

DESIGN SIZE
The completed sachet measures
19 x 11cm (7½ x 4½in)

MATERIALS
**Madeira 6-strand cotton embroidery
thread, 10m (11yd) spiral packs:**
1 x white; 0110 yellow; 0306 peach; 0404
pink; 0412 dark pink; 0901 light lavender;
0902 lavender; 0910 blue; 1001 pale blue;
1006 navy; 1112 aquamarine; 1201 green;
1912 brown
21 x 25cm (8½ x 10in) piece of DMC 18-
count, white Aida fabric
25cm (10in) length of pre-gathered,
white, 3cm (1¼in) wide lace trim
30cm (12in) length of white, 1cm (⅜in)
wide satin ribbon
Sufficient lavender or pot pourri to half
fill the sachet

TO STITCH
The original design was worked in cross
stitch and finished with backstitch. Use
two strands of the thread for the cross
stitches and one strand for embroidery.

Before stitching, fold the fabric in half
widthways and mark the centre line with
basting stitches. Position the design on
the left half of the fabric with the right
side of the motif adjoining the centre
line. The bottom of the design should be
2.5cm (1in) from the bottom of the fabric.

KEY
◣ white		▲ 0902	lavender
☑ 0110	yellow	+ 0910	blue
• 0306	peach	– 1001	pale blue
○ 0404	pink	∕ 1112	aquamarine
⊠ 0412	dark pink	✕ 1201	green
◪ 0901	light lavender	T 1912	brown

EMBROIDERY
0910 blue backstitch for lettering
1006 navy backstitch for all outlines

TO MAKE THE SACHET
1 Fold the embroidered fabric in half
widthways, right sides facing in.
Machine stitch the sides together taking
a 1cm (½in) seam allowance. Trim the
seams and turn the bag right sides out.
Make a 4cm (1½in) single turning on the
top edge and sew.
2 For the trim, join the short edges
together using a neat french seam. Pin
and sew the trim neatly to the inside of
the top edge and, working from the right
side, machine stitch in place, sewing
close to the top edge.
3 Fill the sachet with lavender or pot
pourri and tie the ribbon around the top,
finishing with a bow in the centre.

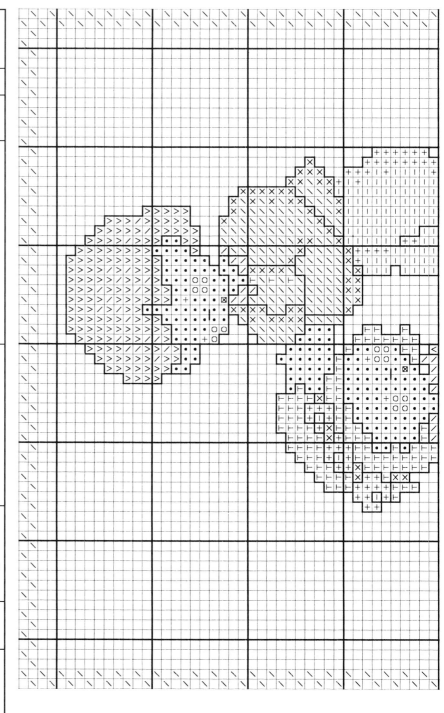

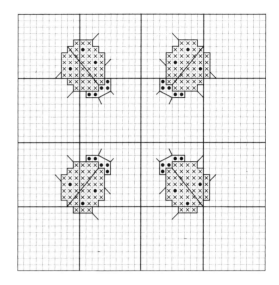

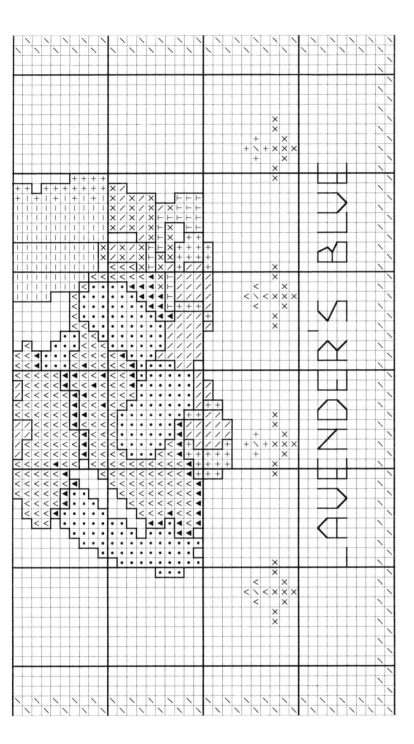

LAVENDER'S BLUE

Ladybird, Ladybird

Illustrated on page 20

MATERIALS
Madeira 6-strand cotton embroidery
thread, 10m (11yd) spiral packs:
2 x 0210 red
1 x black
Remnants of DMC 14-count waste fabric
White romper suit
White padders

TO STITCH
The original design was worked in cross
stitch and finished with backstitch. Use
three strands of the thread for the cross
stitches and two strands for embroidery.

This design is worked using waste fabric
to act as a stitch guide. The waste fabric
is tacked in place wherever you choose
your design to appear, the motif is
stitched, and then the waste fabric is
carefully removed. For this design, the
ladybirds are freely positioned wherever
you choose.

Cut the waste canvas to 2.5cm (1in)
squares, tack in place on the romper suit
and padders, and work the design. Once
the cross stitch is complete, begin cutting
away the excess waste canvas around the
stitched motif. Leave the thread ends
which run behind the cross stitch long
enough to pull out. Gently pull out each
of these threads, one by one.

KEY
⊠ 0210 red ⊡ black

EMBROIDERY
black backstitch for all outlines

I Have Built a Little House

Illustrated on page 22

DESIGN SIZE
20 x 22cm (8 x 8½in)

MATERIALS
Paterna yarn, 8yd skein packs:
3 x 542 cobalt blue
2 x 683 peacock green
1 x 221 charcoal; 261 cream; 433 chocolate
brown; 592 caribbean blue; 771 sunny
yellow; 801 marigold; 941 cranberry
**25 x 27cm (10 x 10½in) piece of DMC 10-
count, white interlock canvas**

TO STITCH
The original design was worked in tent
stitch and finished off with backstitch.
Use three strands of the thread for the
tent stitch, and two strands for the
embroidery. Position the design so that
its centre is at the centre of the canvas.

KEY
● 221 charcoal   · 683 peacock
⊟ 261 cream   green
Λ 433 chocolate brown ○ 771 sunny yellow
☐ 542 cobalt blue   ☑ 801 marigold
⊘ 592 caribbean blue   ☒ 941 cranberry

EMBROIDERY
221 charcoal backstitch for all outlines

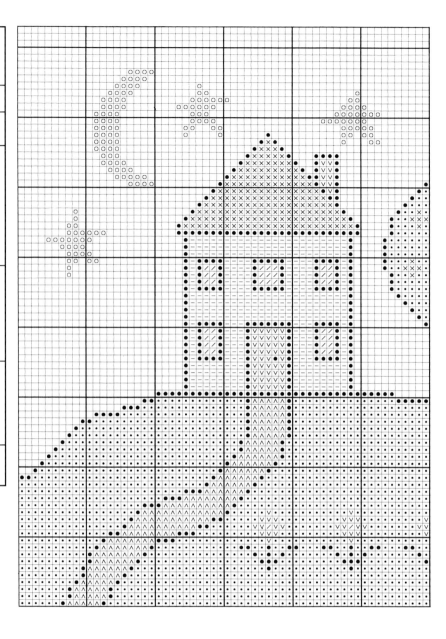

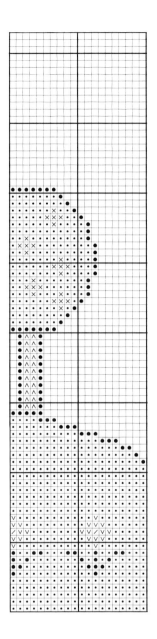

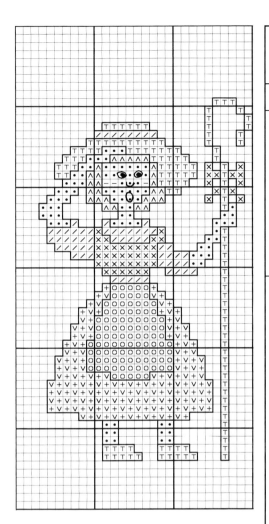

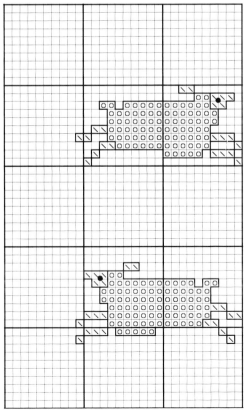

Little Bo Peep

Illustrated on page 21

MATERIALS

Madeira 6-strand cotton embroidery thread, 10m (11yd) spiral packs:
2 x ecru
1 x 0109 yellow; 0210 red; 0306 flesh; 0404 plush; 1006 navy; 1213 mid-green; 1713 charcoal; 1801 mid-grey; 1912 mink; 2008 mid-brown
For Little Bo Peep: 11.5 x 8cm (4½ x 3¼in) piece of DMC 14-count waste canvas
For each sheep: 6.5 x 4cm (2½ x 1½in) piece of DMC 14-count waste canvas
Child's dress

TO STITCH

The original design was worked in cross stitch and finished with backstitch. Use three strands of the thread for the cross stitches and two strands for embroidery. If you are making the dress, it is easier to work the motifs on flat pieces of fabric before making it up.

This design is worked using waste fabric to act as a stitch guide. The waste fabric is tacked in place wherever you choose your design to appear, the motif is stitched, and then the waste fabric is carefully removed. For this design, Little Bo Peep is positioned on the right-hand side of the yoke. The sheep facing right have been positioned around the edge of the hem. They have also been stitched on each collar (using both sheep provided to the left)

Cut the waste canvas to the following sizes:
11.6 x 8cm (4½ x 3¼in) for Little Bo Peep
6.5 x 4cm (2½ x 1½in) for each sheep

Tack the waste canvas to the dress and work the cross stitch through both layers.

Once the cross stitch is complete, begin cutting away the excess waste canvas around the stitched motif. Leave the thread ends which run behind the cross stitch long enough to pull out. Gently pull out each of these threads, one by one.

KEY

○	ecru	☑	1006 navy
╱	0109 yellow	⊞	1213 mid-green
☒	0210 red	╲	1801 mid-grey
•	0306 flesh	△	1912 mink
─	0404 blush	T	2008 mid-brown

EMBROIDERY

1713 charcoal backstitch for all outlines

TO MAKE THE STOCKING

1 Take the back piece of the Aida and working on the right side hand sew the piping around the outer edge leaving a 1cm (½in) seam allowance. Make the loop for the top of the stocking by cutting out a piece of Aida fabric measuring 15 x 4cm (6 x 1½in). Turn in the long edges, hem in place and fold in half to form the loop. Working on the right side of the back, tack the loop to the top outer edge of the stocking with the raw edges placed at an angle. Ensure the loop is facing towards the middle of the stocking. If it is facing outwards it will disappear inside the lining once the lining is attached.

2 With a 1cm (½in) seam allowance and right sides facing, stitch the two pieces of Aida together, leaving the top edge open. Trim the seam allowance and clip into the curves. Turn right sides out.

3 To make the lining, use the same template as for the Aida fabric, and cut out two pieces of batting and lining materials. Take a piece of batting and its matching piece of lining and stitch together all the way around, with the right side of the lining out. Repeat for the other pieces of batting and lining. Then, with a 1cm (½in) seam allowance and right sides facing, stitch the front and back together, leaving the top edge open. Trim the seam allowance and clip into the curves.

4 To attach the lining, slip the Aida fabric stocking inside the lining stocking (right sides facing) and stitch the two together along the top with a 1cm (½in) seam allowance. Trim the seam allowance and corners and turn the lining inside the Aida fabric stocking. Stitch the piping in place.

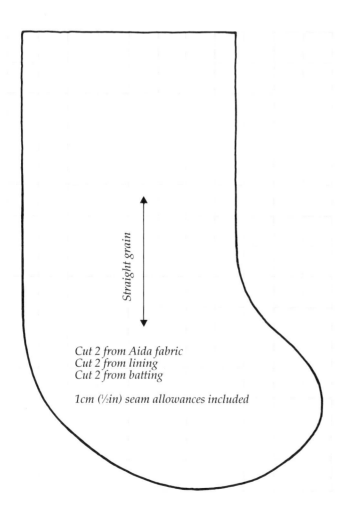

Straight grain

Cut 2 from Aida fabric
Cut 2 from lining
Cut 2 from batting

1cm (½in) seam allowances included

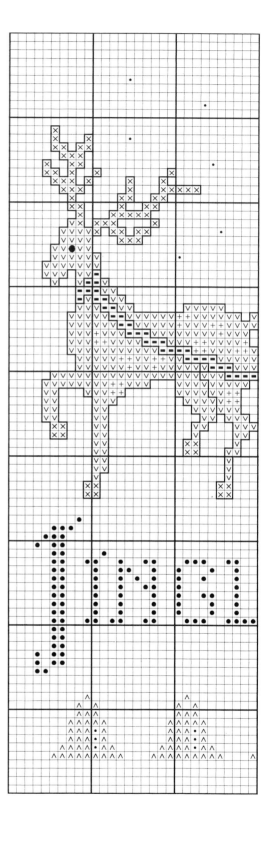

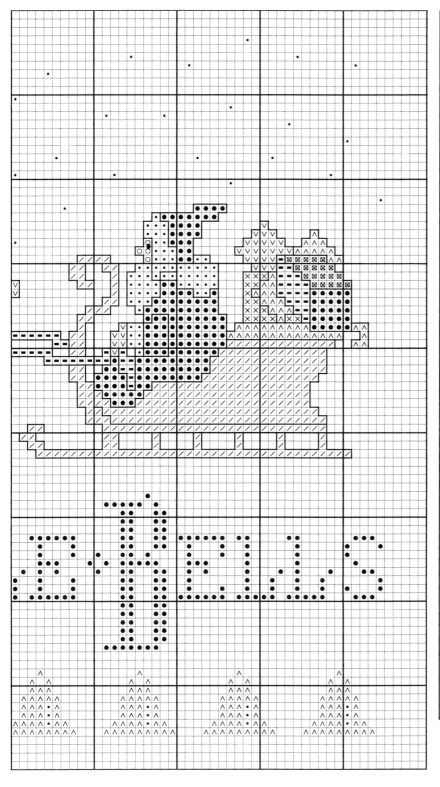

Jingle Bells

Illustrated on page 23

DESIGN SIZE
The completed stocking measures
25 x 35cm (10 x 14in)

MATERIALS
**Madeira 6-strand cotton embroidery
thread, 10m (11yd) spiral packs:**
1 x white; 0201 orange; 0211 red; 0512
crimson; 1711 blue; 1803 grey; 1911 mink;
2011 coffee; 2013 light coffee; 2309 flesh;
black
**Two 27 x 38cm (11 x 15in) pieces of DMC
14-count, dark green Aida fabric
Two 27 x 38cm (11 x 15in) pieces of
lightweight cotton batting
Two 27 x 38cm (11 x 15in) pieces of red
lining material
1m (1yd) red cotton piping**

TO STITCH
The original design was worked in cross
stitch and finished with backstitch. Use
three strands of the thread for the cross
stitches and two strands for embroidery.

Before beginning to stitch, first draw the
stocking template (opposite) to its correct
size (1 square = 2.5cm [1in]) on a piece of
card. Cut out the template, position on
the Aida fabric on the straight grain,
draw around it and cut out two stocking
pieces.

Taking one of the pieces of fabric,
position the motif so that the top of the
design is approximately 7.5cm (3in)
down from the top of the stocking and
the whole is centred to the stocking
width.

KEY
⊡ white		⊠ 1911 mink	
⊠ 0201 orange		☑ 2011 coffee	
● 0211 red		⊞ 2013 light	
▬ 0512 crimson			coffee
⊘ 1711 blue		⊙ 2309 flesh	
⋀ 1803 grey		▣ black	

EMBROIDERY
black backstitch for all outlines
black french knot for Father Christmas's
eye

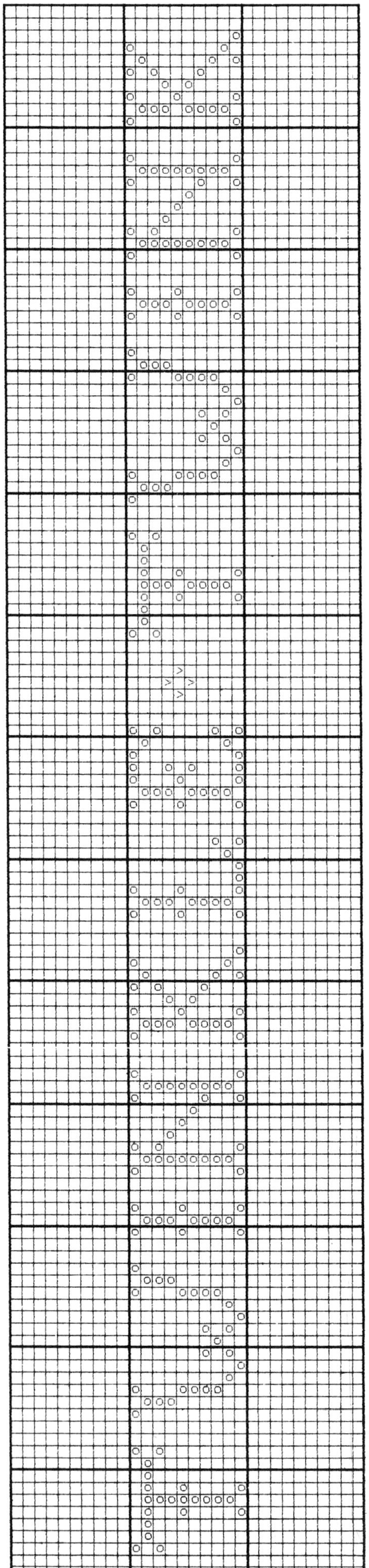

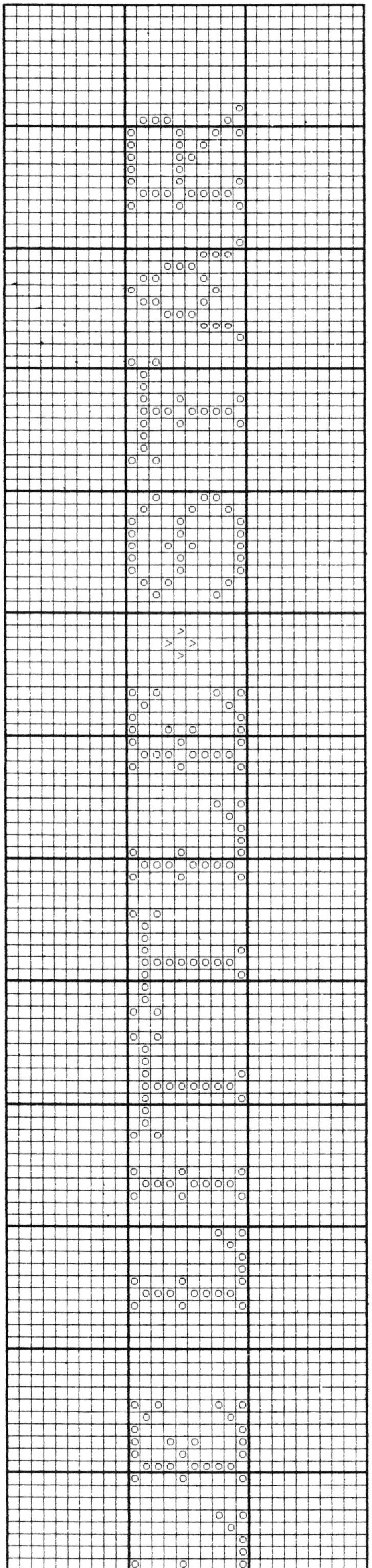

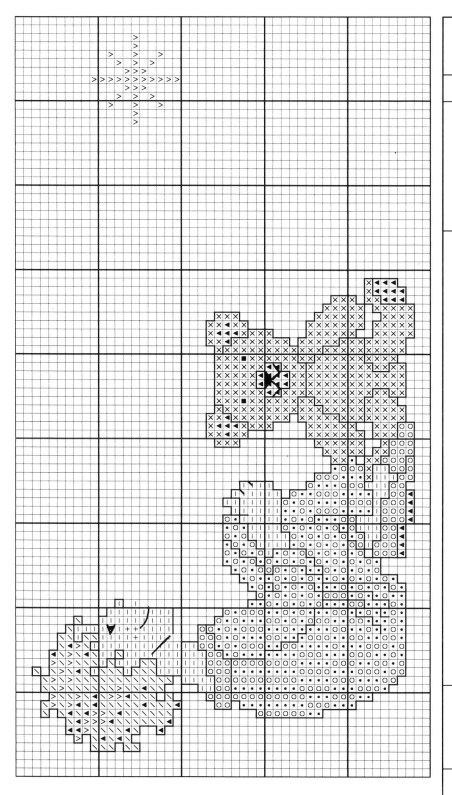

Twinkle, Twinkle, Little Star

Illustrated on page 24

MATERIALS

Madeira 6-strand cotton embroidery thread, 10m (11yd) spiral packs:
1 x white; 0113 yellow; 0404 blush; 1002 pale blue; 1810 charcoal; 2011 coffee; 2211 gold; 2214 dark gold; 2309 flesh
66 x 25cm (26 x 10in) piece of DMC 10-count waste fabric
Blue single sheet
Blue pillow case

TO STITCH

The original design was worked in cross stitch and finished with backstitch. Use three strands of the thread for the cross stitches and two strands for embroidery.

This design is worked using waste fabric to act as a stitch guide. The waste fabric is tacked in place wherever you choose your design to appear, the motif is stitched, and then the waste fabric is carefully removed. For this design, the boy with the teddy is placed at the bottom left corner of the pillow case and the star at the top right corner. The Twinkle, Twinkle, Little Star lettering is placed on the top of the sheet, remembering that the sheet is folded over at the top to the right side.

Cut the waste canvas to the following sizes:
16 x 14cm (6¼ x 5½in) for the boy and teddy motif
4 x 4cm (1½ x 1½in) for the star
66 x 4cm (26 x 1½in) for Twinkle, Twinkle, Little Star.

Tack the waste canvas to the pillow case and sheet and work the cross stitch through both layers.

Once the cross stitch is complete, begin cutting away the excess waste canvas around the stitched motif. Leave the thread ends which run behind the cross stitch long enough to pull out. Gently pull out each of these threads, one by one.

KEY

·	white	⊠	2011 coffee
☑	0113 yellow	◿	2211 gold
⊞	0404 blush	▲	2214 dark gold
◉	1002 pale blue	⊟	2309 flesh
▪	1810 charcoal		

EMBROIDERY

1810 charcoal backstitch for all outlines

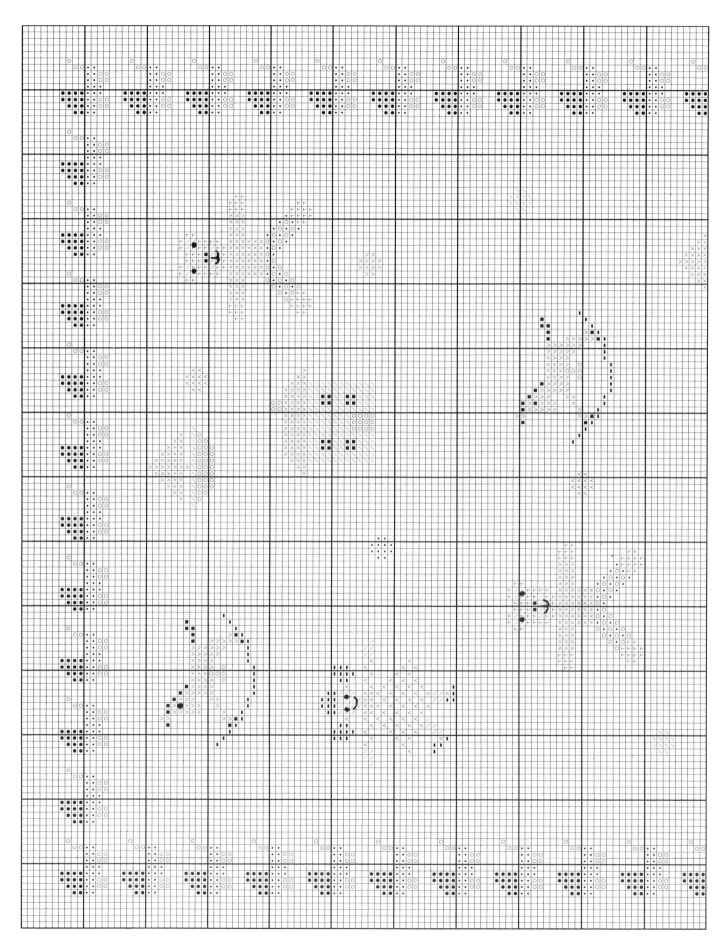

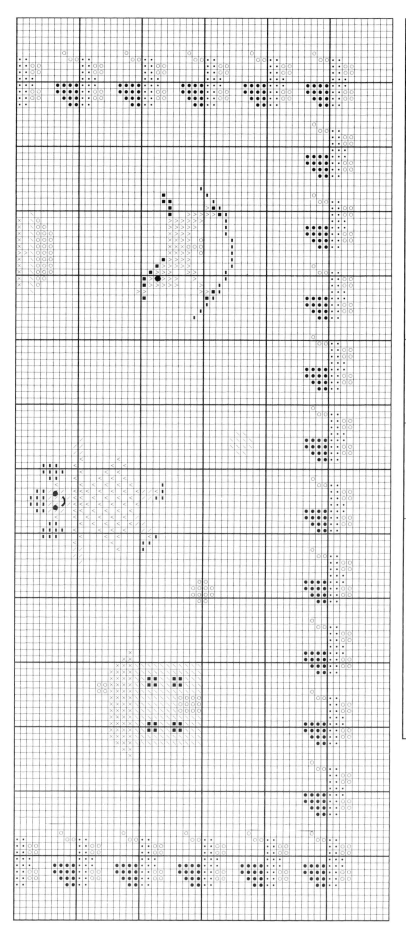

Miss Polly Had a Dolly

Illustrated on page 26

DESIGN SIZE
30 x 25cm (12 x 10in)

MATERIALS
Madeira 6-strand cotton embroidery thread, 10m (11yd) spiral packs:
1 x 0210 red; 0305 flesh; 0605 pink; 0909 light blue; 0911 mid-blue; 1213 green; 1006 navy; 1801 mid-grey; 2009 brown; 2010 coffee; black
33 x 28cm (13 x 11in) piece of DMC 14-count, off-white Aida fabric
122cm (48in) length of off-white, pre-gathered, 2.5cm (1in) wide broderie anglaise edging
32 x 27cm (13 x 11in) piece of medium weight synthetic batting
33 x 28cm (13 x 11in) piece of off-white cotton lining fabric

TO STITCH
The original design was worked in cross stitch. Use three strands of the thread throughout. Position the design so that its centre is at the centre of the Aida fabric.

KEY
☒	0210 red		●	1006 navy
◥	0305 flesh		☑	1801 mid-grey
◿	0605 pink		▬	2009 brown
·	0909 light blue		T	2010 coffee
○	0911 mid-blue		■	black
△	1213 green			

TO MAKE THE COVER
1 Working on the right side and with the raw edge placed just inside the 1cm (½in) seam allowance, baste the lace edging around the outer edge of the embroidery section.
2 Lay the embroidered section face up on a clean surface, lay the batting over it, smoothing it out and matching the edges. Then lay the lining fabric over the batting, right side down, again matching the edges. Pin and then baste the three layers together. Machine stitch leaving a small gap on one side for turning. Trim the seams and corners and turn right sides out with the batting in the middle. Hand stitch the gap.

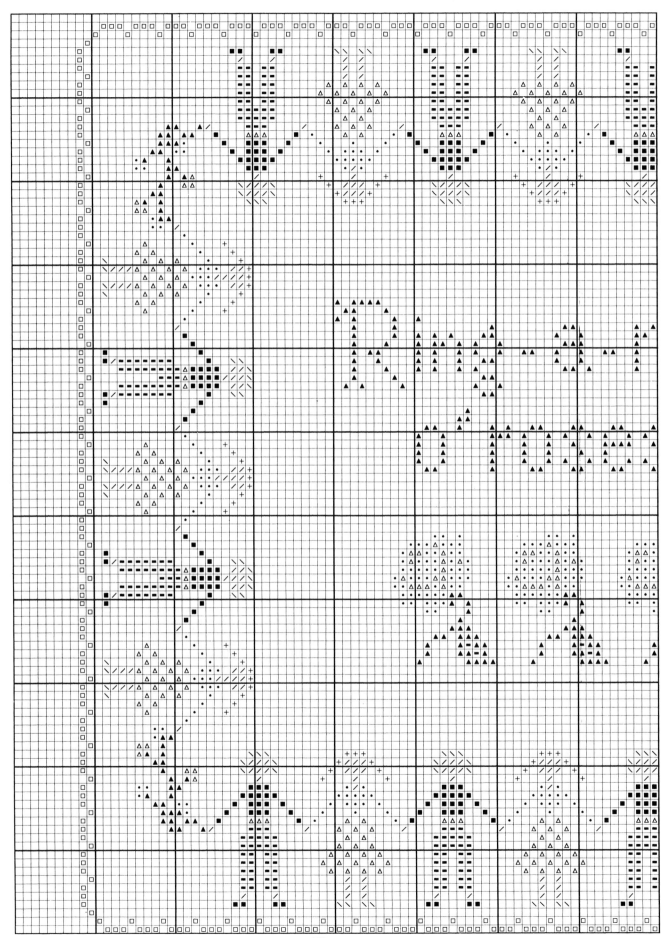

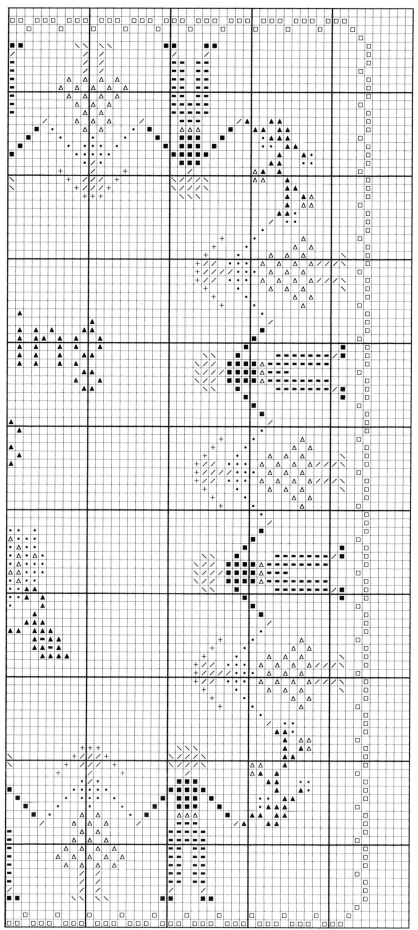

Ring-a-Ring
o' Roses

Illustrated on page 27

DESIGN SIZE
The completed table mat measures
33 x 35cm (13 x 14in)

MATERIALS
**Madeira 6-strand cotton embroidery
thread, 10m (11yd) spiral packs:**
1 x 0109 yellow; 0408 pale pink; 0412 dark
pink; 0501 flesh; 0908 light blue; 0910
mid-blue; 1210 light green; 1213 mid-
green; 2008 brown
**35 x 38cm (14 x 15in) piece of DMC 11-
count, white Aida fabric**

TO STITCH
The original design was worked in cross
stitch. Use three strands of the thread
throughout. Position the design so that
its centre is at the centre of the Aida
fabric.

KEY
⊞ 0109	yellow	■ 0910	mid-blue
⊡ 0408	pale pink	⊟ 1210	light green
△ 0412	dark pink	▲ 1213	mid-green
⊿ 0501	flesh	◻ 2008	brown
▢ 0908	light blue		

TO MAKE THE TABLE MAT
1 When the embroidery is complete,
trim it very carefully to the finished size
of 33 x 35cm (13 x 14in).
2 To make a fringe, work a line of zigzag
machine stitching 2cm (¾in) in from the
edge. Then pull out the threads up to
this line.

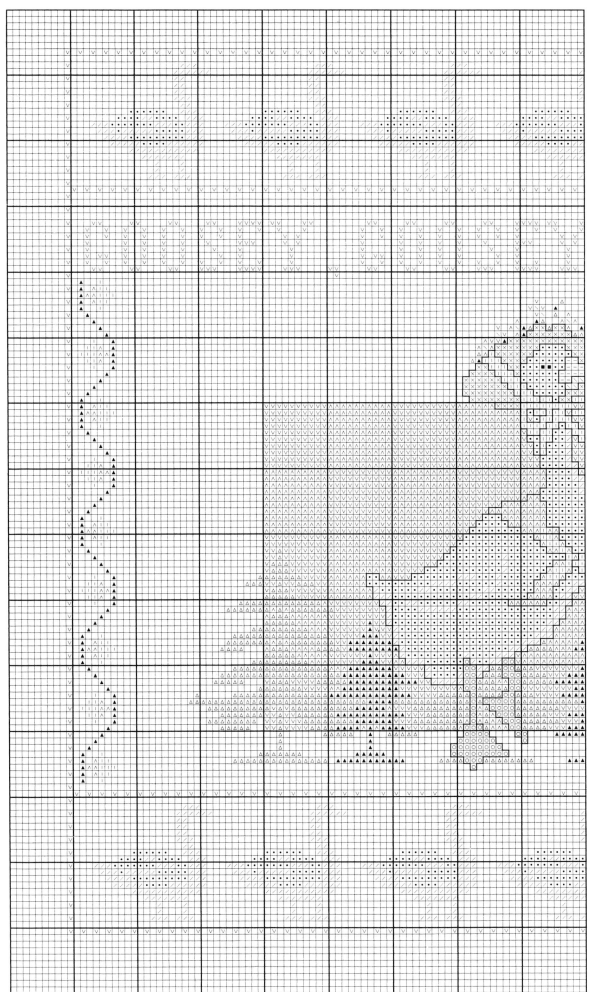

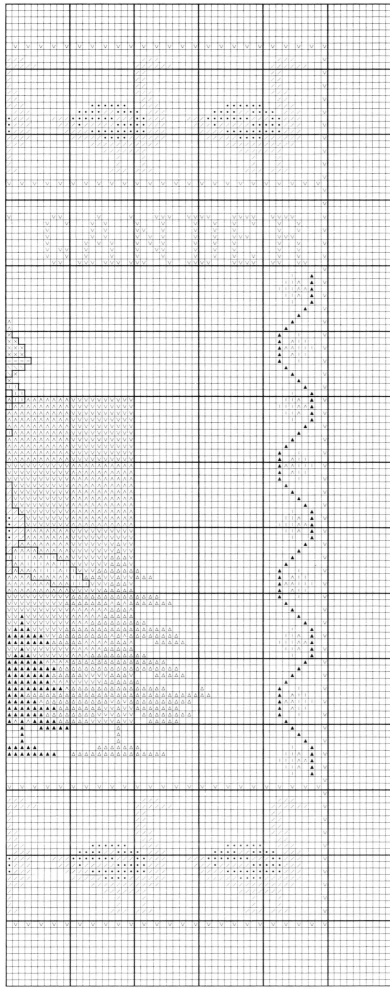

Goosey, Goosey Gander

Illustrated on page 28

DESIGN SIZE
33 x 34cm (13 x 13½in)

MATERIALS
Paterna yarn, 8yd skein packs:
8 x 505 mid-federal blue
2 x 220 black; 500 dark federal blue; 772 light sunny yellow; 812 sunrise; 842 salmon; 906 American beauty pink; 941 cranberry
1 x 212 pearl grey; 260 white; 661 pine green; 662 light pine green; 771 sunny yellow
38 x 39cm (15 x 15½in) piece of DMC 10-count, white interlock canvas
35 x 35cm (14 x 14in) piece of backing fabric
33 x 34cm (13 x 13½in) cushion pad
30cm (12in) zip (optional)
137cm (54in) contrasting 5mm (¼in) piping cord

TO STITCH
The original design was worked in tent stitch and finished with backstitch. Use two strands of the thread for the tent stitches and one strand for embroidery. Position the design so that its centre is at the centre of the canvas.

KEY
◹ 212	pearl grey	⊟ 771	sunny yellow
◼ 220	black		
⊡ 260	white	⊠ 772	light sunny yellow
☑ 500	dark federal blue	◥ 812	sunrise
☐ 505	mid-federal blue	⊙ 842	salmon
▲ 661	pine green	◭ 906	American beauty pink
△ 662	light pine green	⊡ 941	cranberry

EMBROIDERY
220 black backstitch for all outlines

TO MAKE THE CUSHION COVER
1 With right sides facing, stitch the embroidered front and backing fabric together leaving a 30cm (12in) opening in the middle of one side. Trim across the corners and turn the cover right sides out.
2 Insert the cushion, turn in the edges of the opening and slipstitch, or insert the zip, to close.
3 Pin the piping around the edges and stitch in place.

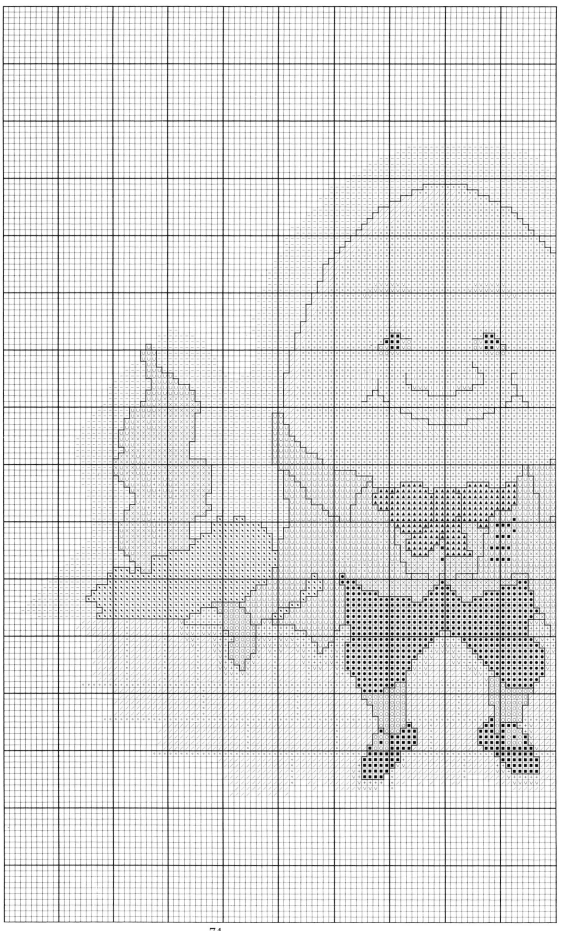

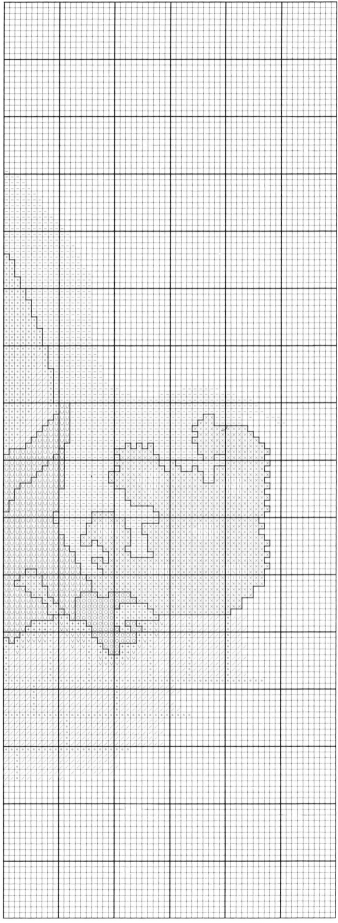

Humpty Dumpty

Illustrated on page 29

DESIGN SIZE
38 x 38cm (15 x 15in)

MATERIALS
Paterna yarn, 8yd skein packs:
13 x 564 glacier light blue
3 x 563 glacier mid-blue; 405 light fawn
brown
2 x 221 charcoal; 413 light earth brown;
661 dark pine green; 692 mid-loden green
1 x 262 cream; D281 light antique rose;
411 dark earth brown; 412 mid-earth
brown; 511 old blue; 612 mid-hunter
green; 941 cranberry; 952 strawberry
**41 x 41cm (16 x 16in) piece of DMC 10-
count, white interlock canvas**

TO STITCH
The original design was worked in tent
stitch and finished with backstitch. Use
three strands of the thread for the tent
stitches and two strands for embroidery.
Position the design so that its centre is
at the centre of the canvas.

KEY
■	221 charcoal	⊟	563 glacier mid-blue
◯	262 cream		
Ⅱ	D281 light antique rose	☐	564 glacier light blue
◎	405 light fawn brown	◥	612 mid-hunter green
+	411 dark earth brown	U	661 dark pine green
☑	412 mid-earth brown	☒	692 mid-loden green
⧄	413 light earth brown	▲	941 cranberry
●	511 old blue	◺	952 strawberry

EMBROIDERY
221 charcoal backstitch for all outlines

TO MAKE THE FOOTSTOOL
Follow the manufacturer's instructions
for assembling the footstool.
Note that although the finished footstool
is 38 x 38cm (15 x 15in) you need to stitch
a square measuring 40 x 40cm (16 x 16in)
to allow for fixing in place. This is the size
of this chart.

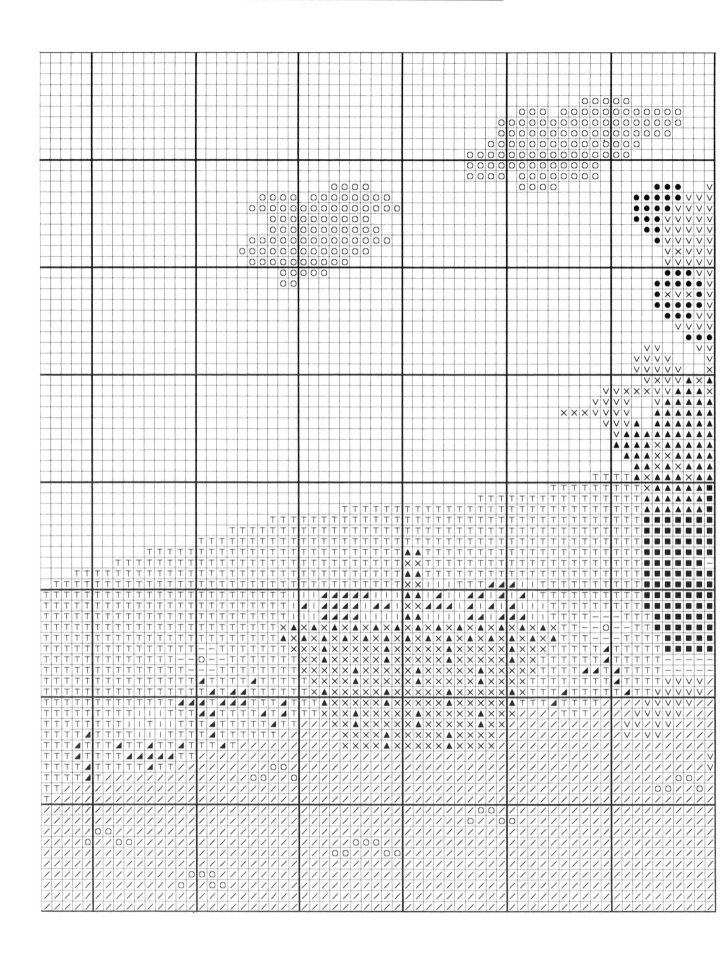

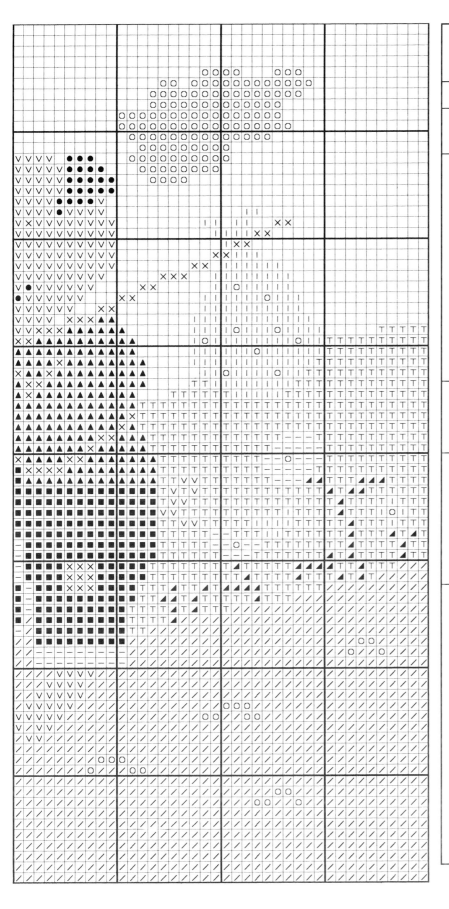

This Little Piggy Went to Market

Illustrated on page 30

DESIGN SIZE
The completed bag measures
19 x 14cm (7 ½ x 5 ½ in)

MATERIALS
Paterna yarn, 8yd skein packs:
2 x 564 glacier light blue
1 x 263 cream; 424 coffee brown; 453
khaki brown; 463 beige brown; 511 old
blue; 512 light old blue; 612 hunter green;
691 loden green; 932 mid-rusty rose; 934
light rusty rose; 951 strawberry
24 x 19cm (9½ x 7½in) piece of DMC 14-
count, white interlock canvas
24 x 19cm (9½ x 7½in) piece of toning
lining cotton
24 x 19cm (9½ x 7½in) piece of toning
fabric for the backing
49 x 7.5cm (19½ x 3in) piece of toning
fabric for the gusset
114cm (45in) narrow cord
18cm (7in) zip

TO STITCH
The original design was worked in tent
stitch. Use two strands of the thread
throughout. Position the design so that
its centre is at the centre of the canvas.

KEY

⊙	263 cream	☐	564 glacier
☒	424 coffee brown		light blue
▲	453 khaki brown	⊤	612 hunter
◪	463 beige brown		green
■	511 old blue	◢	691 loden
⊟	512 light old blue		green
☑	934 light rusty rose	⊙	932 mid-rusty
			rose
		⊡	951 strawberry

TO MAKE THE SHOULDER PURSE
1 Trim the canvas to within five single
threads of the embroidery. Line the
embroidery with a piece of lining cut to
the same size. Trim the backing fabric to
the same size as the front.
2 Attach the zip first to the top edge of
the canvas and then to the back. Open
the zip.
3 Right sides facing, stitch the back of
the purse to the gusset, and then stitch
the front to the gusset. Turn the purse
through to the right side.
4 Sew the cord around the front edge of
the bag, stitching the raw ends to the
inside of the purse. Make the strap by
sewing the looped ends of a length of
cord to each side.
5 Make two tabs for the zip by cutting
two 2.5cm (1in) squares from the backing
fabric. Hem the edges, fold in half and
sew one at each end of the zip.

TO MAKE THE BAG

1 Cut out the cotton fabric pieces as indicated in the diagrams (below).

2 For the lining, with right sides facing, join two of pieces D at one side seam and stitch in place taking a 1cm (½in) seam allowance. Fold one piece of C in half and mark the sides with contrasting thread. With right sides of C and the Ds together, start pinning at side, matching the side marks. Continue until the welt is pinned right round the base. Stitch the pinned seam taking a 1cm (½in) seam allowance. Taking care, snip V-shaped notches very near stitching at 2cm (¾in) intervals around the seam and press the turnings onto the welt. With right sides facing, join the remaining side seam.

3 For the piping, cut strips of the cotton fabric on the bias and wrap around the cord. The strips need to be sufficiently wide to wrap around the cord and leave a 1cm (½in) seam allowance. Pin onto the remaining piece of C on the right side so that the edges of the piping lie on the edge of the circle.

4 For the bag, with right sides facing, join two of the B pieces to one of the A, above and below (see photograph, page 30). With right sides facing, join BAB to the remaining piece of D at one side and stitch in place taking a 1cm (½in) seam allowance. Fold the remaining piece of C in half and mark the sides with contrasting thread. With right sides of C and the BABs together, start pinning at side, matching the side marks. Continue until the welt is pinned right round the base. Stitch the pinned seam taking a 1cm (½in) seam allowance. Taking care, snip V-shaped notches very near stitching at 2cm (¾in) intervals around the seam and press the turnings onto the welt. With right sides facing, join the remaining side seam.

5 With right sides facing, join lining to outside of bag at top and stitch. Trim the seams and turn, right sides out.

6 On the front of the bag make one 2.5cm (1in) wide eyelet hole through both the bag and the lining. It should be positioned 3cm (1¼in) in from the side seams and 7.5cm (3in) down from the top of the bag. Repeat on the back.

7 To make a drawstring panel, machine stitch twice right around the bag, once 1cm (½in) above the eyelet holes and again 1cm (½in) below the eyelet holes. Insert the drawstring cord through the drawstring panel using the eyelets. Secure the cord.

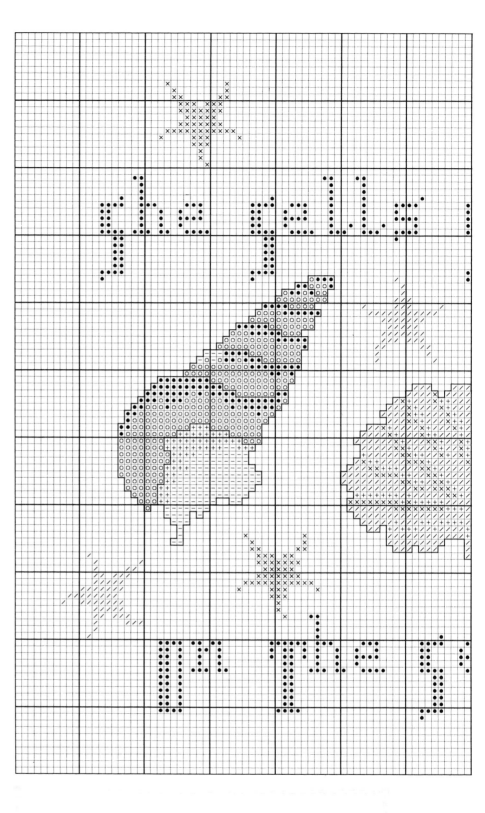

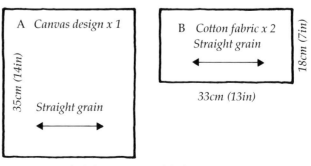

A *Canvas design x 1*

35cm (14in)

Straight grain

33cm (13in)

B *Cotton fabric x 2*
Straight grain

18cm (7in)

33cm (13in)

1cm (½in) seam allowances included

78

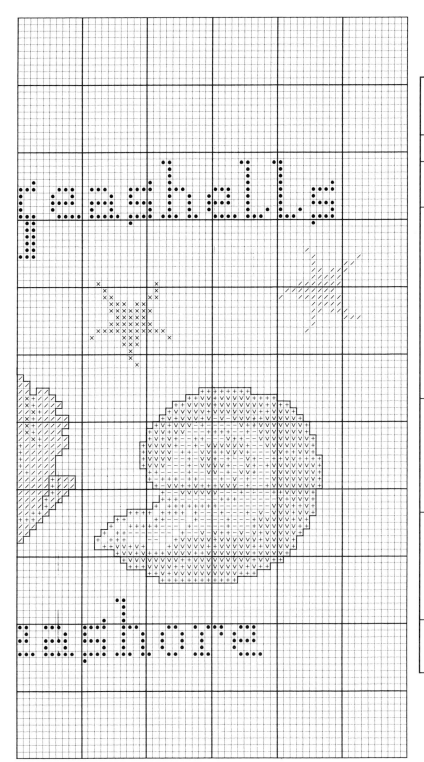

She Sells Sea Shells

Illustrated on page 31

DESIGN SIZE
The completed bag measures
63 x 31cm (25 x 12in)

MATERIALS
Paterna yarn, 8yd skein packs:
12 x 444 golden brown
1 x 462 mid-beige brown; 464 light beige
brown; 502 federal blue; 523 light teal
blue; 752 old gold; 922 dark wood rose;
924 light wood rose
35 x 33cm (14 x 13in) piece of DMC 10-
count, white interlock canvas
100 x 122cm (40 x 48in) piece of medium-
heavyweight cotton fabric (for bag,
lining and piping)
65cm (26in) length of piping cord for the
base
180cm (72in) length of cord for the handle

TO STITCH
The original design was worked in tent
stitch and finished off with backstitch. Use
three strands of the thread for the tent
stitch, and two strands for embroidery.

Before starting to stitch, cut out the
canvas as indicated in the diagrams
(below). Centre the design to the canvas.

KEY
☐ 444 golden brown   ⊙ 523 light teal blue
⊞ 462 mid-beige brown   ☑ 752 old gold
⊟ 464 light beige brown   ☒ 922 dark wood rose
⊡ 502 federal blue   ⊘ 924 light wood rose

EMBROIDERY
462 mid-beige brown backstitch
for all outlines

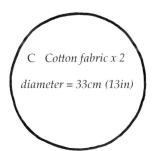

C   Cotton fabric x 2

diameter = 33cm (13in)

1cm (½in) seam allowances included

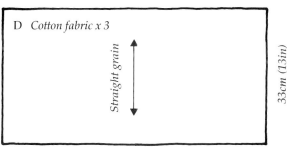

D   Cotton fabric x 3

Straight grain

33cm (13in)

65cm (26in)

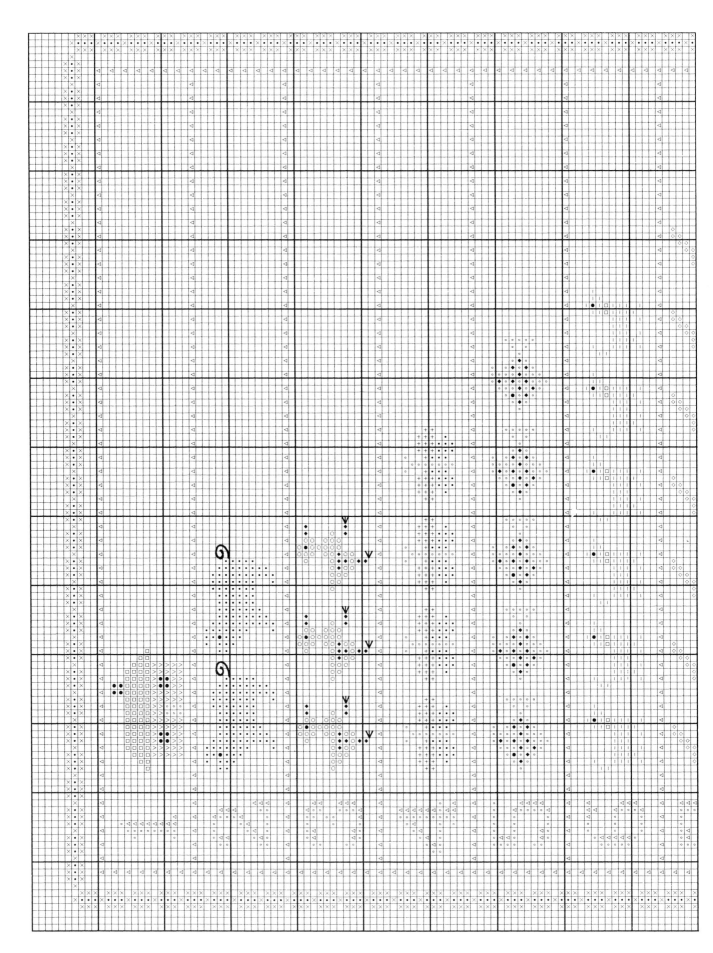

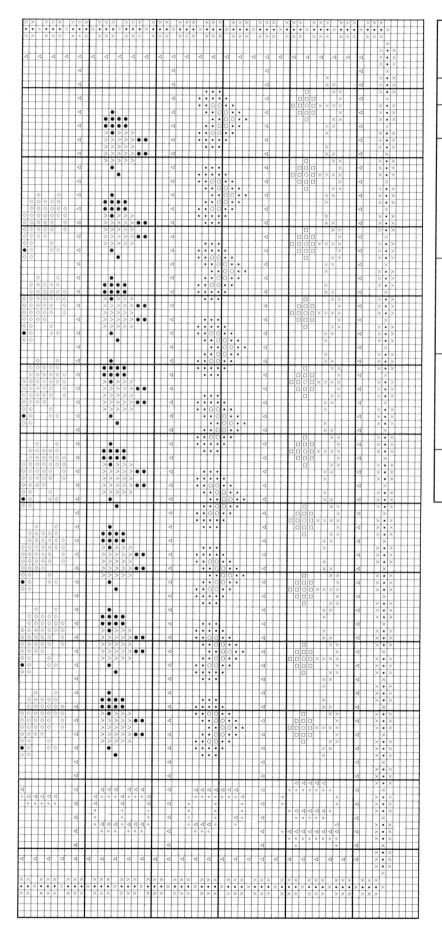

Nursery Numbers

Illustrated on page 32

DESIGN SIZE
23 x 27.5cm (9 x 10¾in)

MATERIALS
Madeira 6-strand cotton embroidery thread, 10m (11yd) spiral packs:
1 x white; 0106 yellow; 0206 orange; 0210 red; 0414 pink; 0712 purple; 0909 light blue; 0912 mid-blue; 1408 moss green; 1801 mid-grey; 1914 brown; black
28 x 33cm (11 x 13in) piece of DMC 14-count, beige Aida fabric

TO STITCH
The original design was worked in cross stitch and finished with backstitch. Use three strands of the thread for the cross stitches and two strands for embroidery. Position the design so that its centre is at the centre of the Aida fabric.

KEY

☑	white	△	0909	light blue
○	0106 yellow	○	0912	mid-blue
◆	0206 orange	✕	1408	moss green
☐	0210 red	◇	1801	mid-grey
·	0414 pink	−	1914	brown
+	0712 purple	●	black	

EMBROIDERY
black backstitch for pig's tails and duck's feet

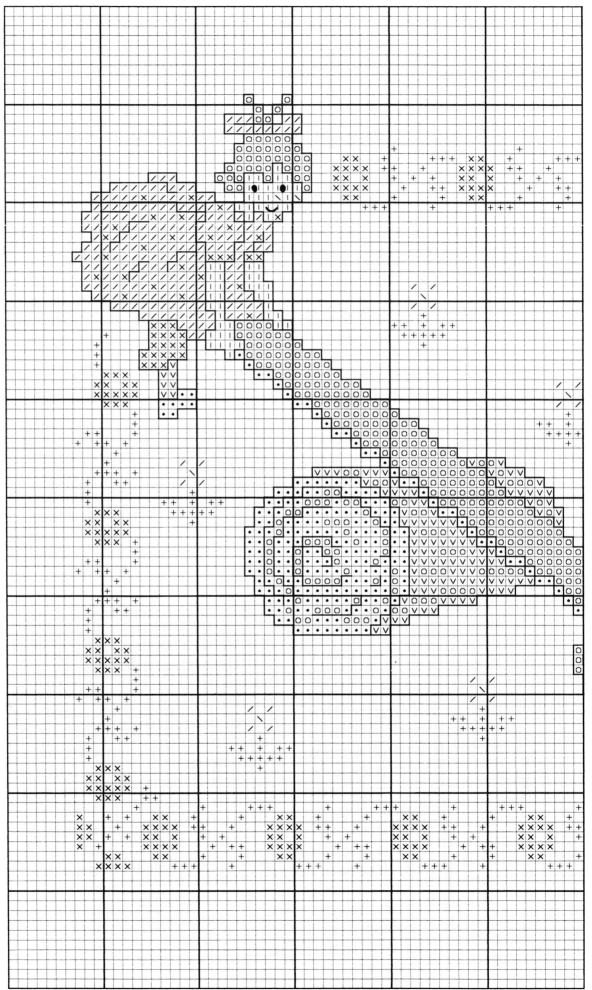

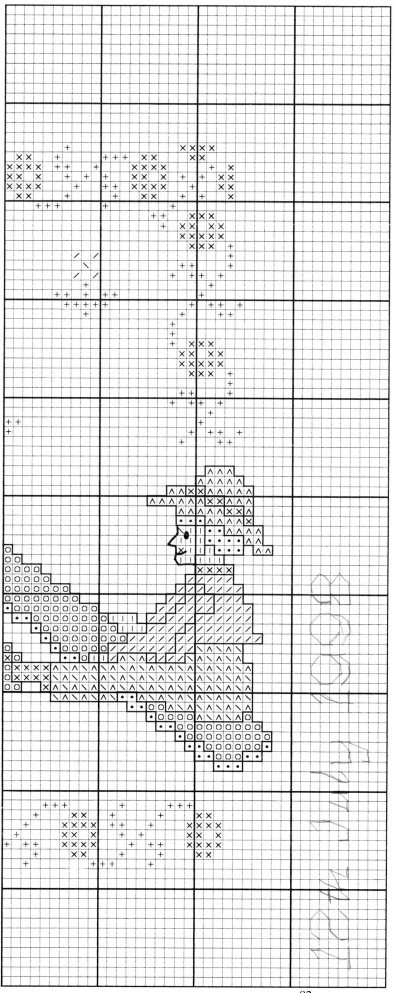

See-Saw, Margery Daw

Illustrated on page 33

DESIGN SIZE
22.5 x 22.5cm (10 x 10in)

MATERIALS
Paterna yarn, 8yd skein packs:
7 x 694 light loden green
1 x 202 steel grey; 221 charcoal; 323 plum;
441 dark golden brown; 442 golden
brown; 550 dark ice blue; 552 ice blue; 690
loden green; 931 rusty rose; 934 light
rusty rose
28 x 28cm (11 x 11in) piece of DMC 10-
count, white interlock canvas

TO STITCH
The original design was worked in tent
stitch and finished off with backstitch.
Use three strands of the thread for the
tent stitch, and one strand for the
embroidery. Position the design so that
its centre is at the centre of the canvas.

KEY

☑	202	steel grey	◿	552 ice blue
◿	323	plum	+	690 loden green
⊙	441	dark golden brown	☐	694 light loden green
·	442	golden brown	⊠	931 rusty rose
◺	550	dark ice blue	⊡	934 light rusty rose

EMBROIDERY
221 charcoal backstitch for all outlines

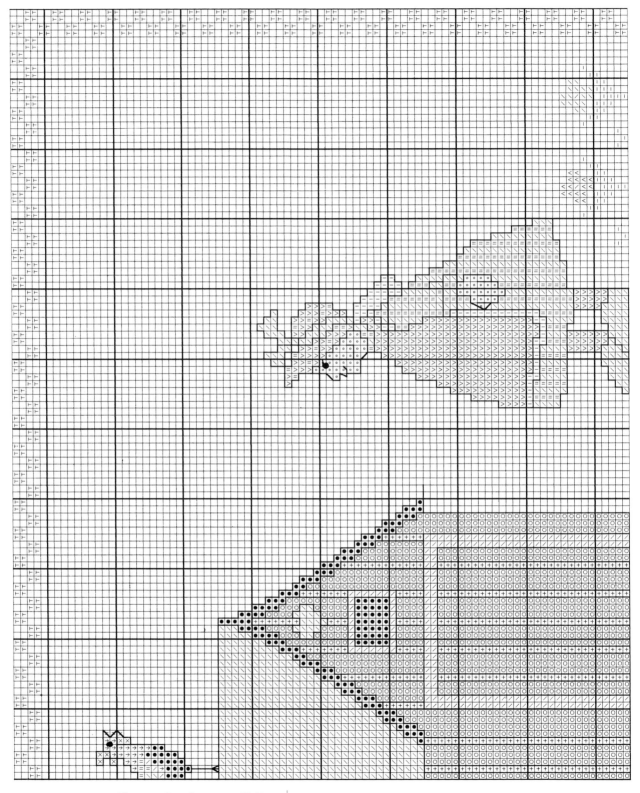

Chart continued on pages 86-7   ↓

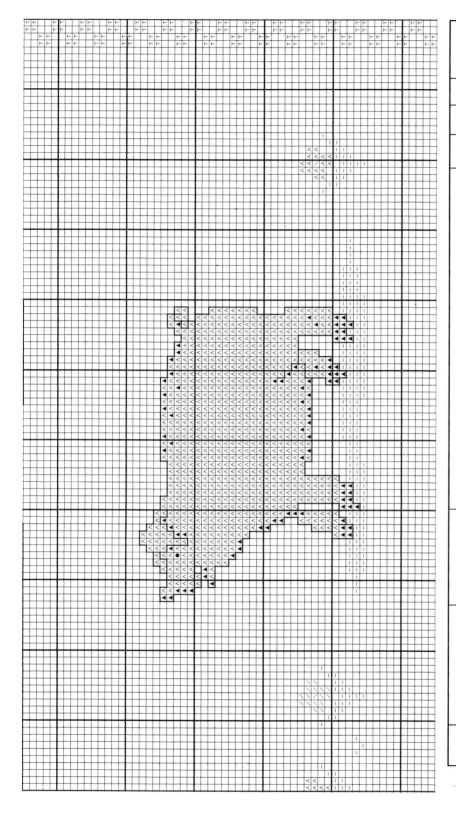

Sleep, Baby, Sleep

COT COVER

Illustrated on page 34

DESIGN SIZE
71 x 50cm (28 x 20in)

MATERIALS
Madeira 6-strand cotton embroidery thread, 10m (11yd) spiral packs:
3 x 1901 light grey
2 x ecru; 1707 slate blue; 1713 charcoal; 2009 coffee
1 x 0107 yellow; 0213 red; 0306 flesh; 0310 orange; 0405 dark pink; 0503 pale pink; 0810 plum; 1107 kingfisher; 1503 moss green; 1911 mink
73 x 52cm (29 x 21in) piece of DMC 11-count, white Aida fabric
73 x 52cm (29 x 21in) piece of medium weight synthetic batting
73 x 52cm (29 x 21in) piece of white cotton lining fabric

To make both the cot cover and bumper you will need the following amounts of Madeira 6-strand cotton embroidery thread, 10m (11yd) spiral packs:
4 x 1901 light grey
3 x ecru; 1713 charcoal; 2009 coffee
2 x 0503 pale pink; 1503 moss green; 1707 slate blue; 1911 mink
1 x 0107 yellow; 0213 red; 0306 flesh; 0310 orange; 0405 dark pink; 0810 plum; 1107 kingfisher

TO STITCH
The original design was worked in cross stitch and finished with backstitch. Use three strands of the thread for the cross stitches and two strands for embroidery. Position the design so that its centre is at the centre of the Aida fabric.

KEY
☑ ecru		◹ 1107 kingfisher	
↓ 0107 yellow		− 1503 moss green	
× 0213 red		⧄ 1707 slate blue	
◦ 0306 flesh		● 1713 charcoal	
‖ 0310 orange		T 1901 light grey	
▲ 0405 dark pink		+ 1911 mink	
⋀ 0503 pale pink		⊡ 2009 coffee	
◌ 0810 plum			

EMBROIDERY
1713 charcoal backstitch for all outlines

→ *Chart continued on pages 88-9*

↑   *Chart continued on pages 84-5*

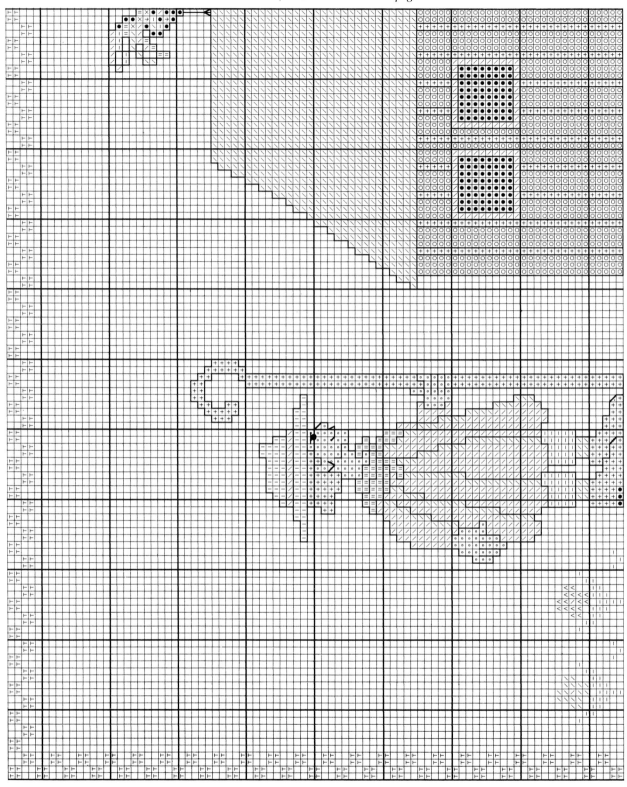

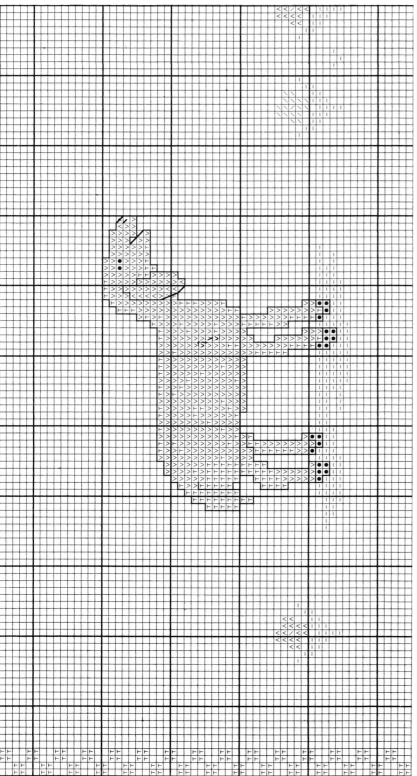

→ *Chart continued on pages 90-1*

KEY

⊻	ecru	◨	1107 kingfisher
↓	0107 yellow	⊟	1503 moss green
⊠	0213 red	☑	1707 slate blue
⊙	0306 flesh	●	1713 charcoal
‖	0310 orange	⊤	1901 light grey
▲	0405 dark pink	⊞	1911 mink
⅄	0503 pale pink	⊡	2009 coffee
⊚	0810 plum		

EMBROIDERY
1713 charcoal backstitch for all outlines

TO MAKE THE COVER
1 Lay the embroidery face up on a clean, flat surface. Carefully lay the batting over the embroidered top, smoothing it out and matching the edges. Lay the backing fabric over the batting, face down, and again match the edges. Pin and then baste the three layers together. Machine stitch taking a 1cm (½in) seam allowance and leaving a small gap on one side for turning the cover through.
2 Trim the seams and corners and turn the cover right sides out. Hand stitch the gap to close it.

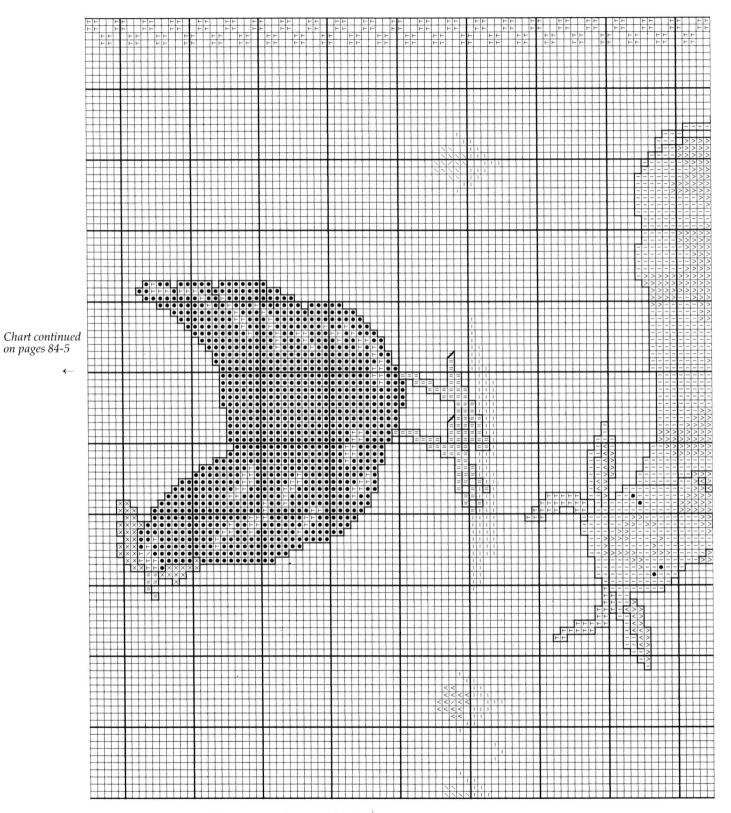

Chart continued on pages 84-5

←

Chart continued on pages 90-1 ↓

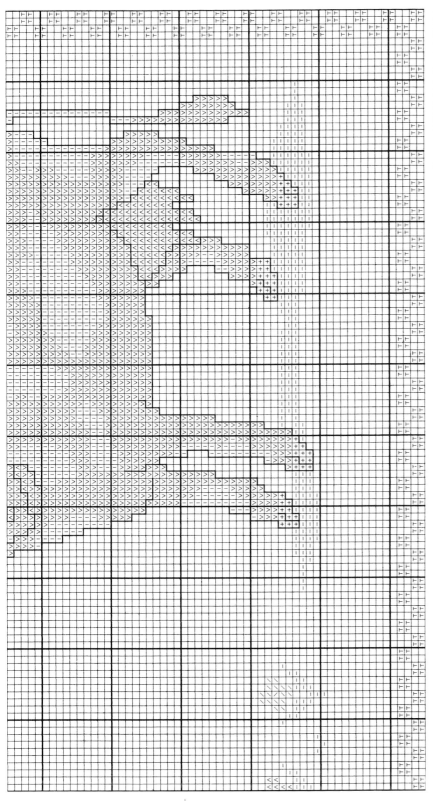

↓ *Chart continued on pages 90-1*

Sleep, Baby, Sleep

COT BUMPER

Illustrated on page 34

DESIGN SIZE
152 x 25cm (60 x 10in)

MATERIALS
Madeira 6-strand cotton embroidery thread, 10m (11yd) spiral packs:
2 x 1713 charcoal
1 x ecru; 0213 red; 0310 orange; 0405 dark pink; 0503 pale pink; 1503 moss green; 1707 slate blue; 1901 light grey; 1 x 2009 coffee
154 x 27cm (61 x 11in) piece of DMC 11-count, white Aida fabric
154 x 27cm (61 x 11in) piece of medium weight synthetic batting
154 x 36cm (61 x 15in) piece of white cotton lining fabric

To make both the cot cover and bumper you will need the following amounts of Madeira 6-strand cotton embroidery thread, 10m (11yd) spiral packs:
4 x 1901 light grey
3 x ecru; 1713 charcoal; 2009 coffee
2 x 0503 pale pink; 1503 moss green; 1707 slate blue; 1911 mink
1 x 0107 yellow; 0213 red; 0306 flesh; 0310 orange; 0405 dark pink; 0810 plum; 1107 kingfisher

TO STITCH
The original design was worked in cross stitch and finished with backstitch. Use three strands of the thread for the cross stitches and two strands for embroidery.

Before stitching, divide the Aida fabric into six equal-sized sections along its length. Baste markers at top and bottom edges to indicate the divisions. Follow the chart as set for the quilt but work the animal motifs only, one centred in each section. Stitch the animals in the following order from left to right: horse, dog, lamb, pig, hen, cow.

KEY
☑	ecru	◣	1107 kingfisher
↓	0107 yellow	–	1503 moss green
☒	0213 red	╱	1707 slate blue
○	0306 flesh	●	1713 charcoal
‖	0310 orange	T	1901 light grey
▲	0405 dark pink	+	1911 mink
△	0503 pale pink	I	2009 coffee
⊙	0810 plum		

EMBROIDERY
1713 charcoal backstitch for all outlines

↑ *Chart continued on pages 88-9*

*Chart continued
on pages 86-7*
←

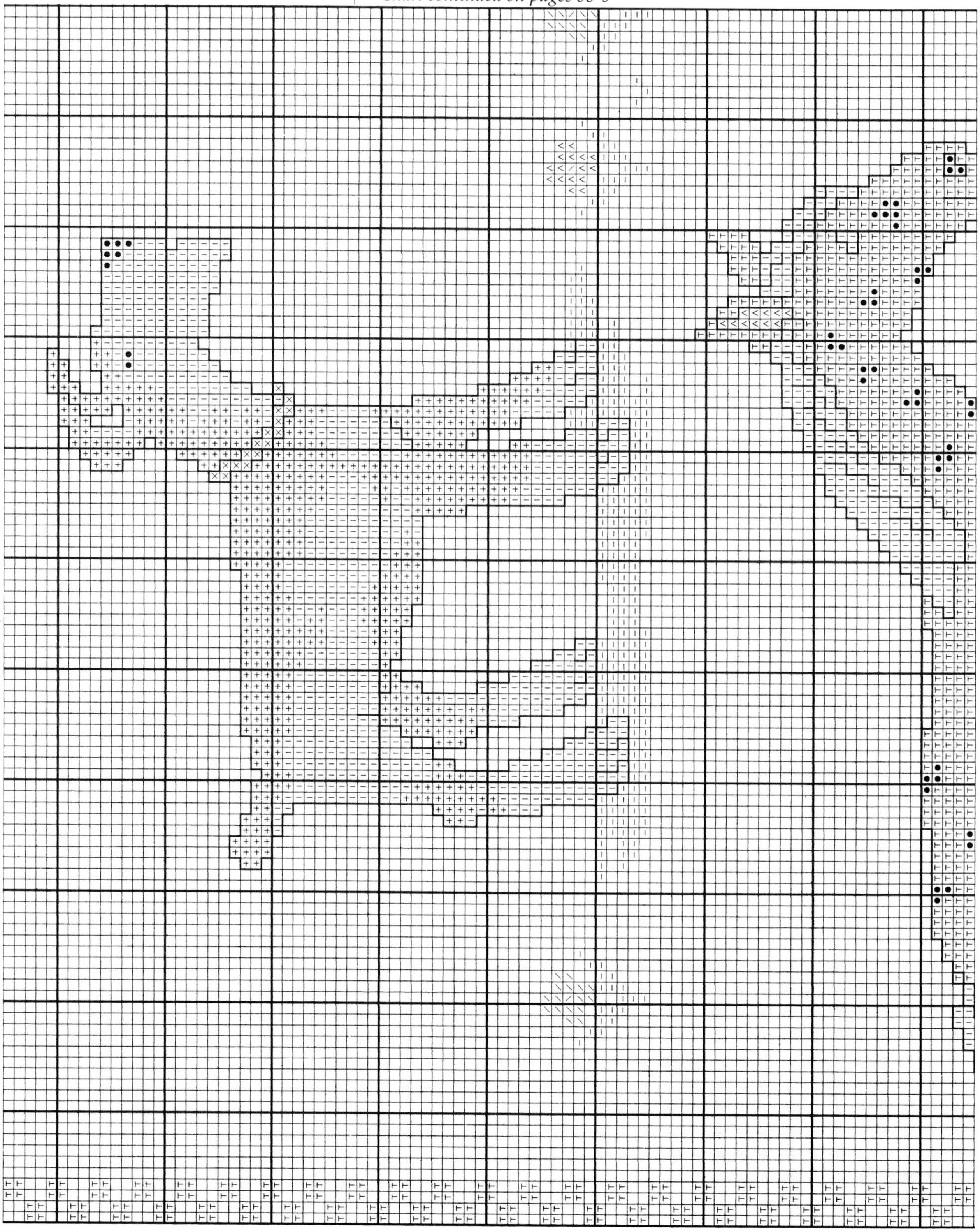

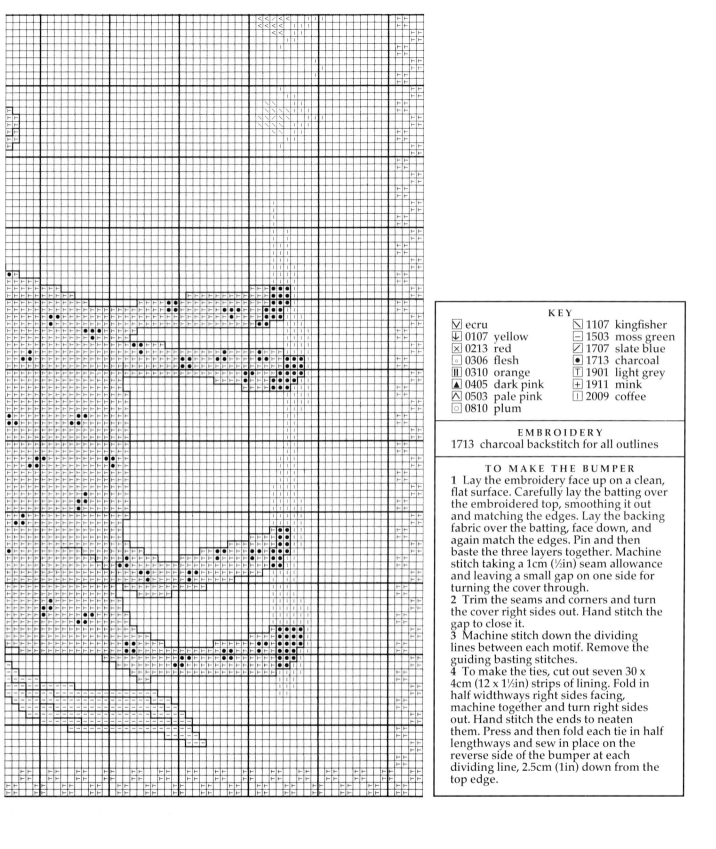

EMBROIDERY
1713 charcoal backstitch for all outlines

TO MAKE THE BUMPER

1 Lay the embroidery face up on a clean, flat surface. Carefully lay the batting over the embroidered top, smoothing it out and matching the edges. Lay the backing fabric over the batting, face down, and again match the edges. Pin and then baste the three layers together. Machine stitch taking a 1cm (½in) seam allowance and leaving a small gap on one side for turning the cover through.

2 Trim the seams and corners and turn the cover right sides out. Hand stitch the gap to close it.

3 Machine stitch down the dividing lines between each motif. Remove the guiding basting stitches.

4 To make the ties, cut out seven 30 x 4cm (12 x 1½in) strips of lining. Fold in half widthways right sides facing, machine together and turn right sides out. Hand stitch the ends to neaten them. Press and then fold each tie in half lengthways and sew in place on the reverse side of the bumper at each dividing line, 2.5cm (1in) down from the top edge.

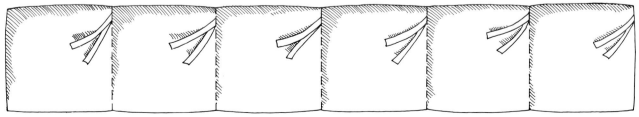

Reverse side of bumper

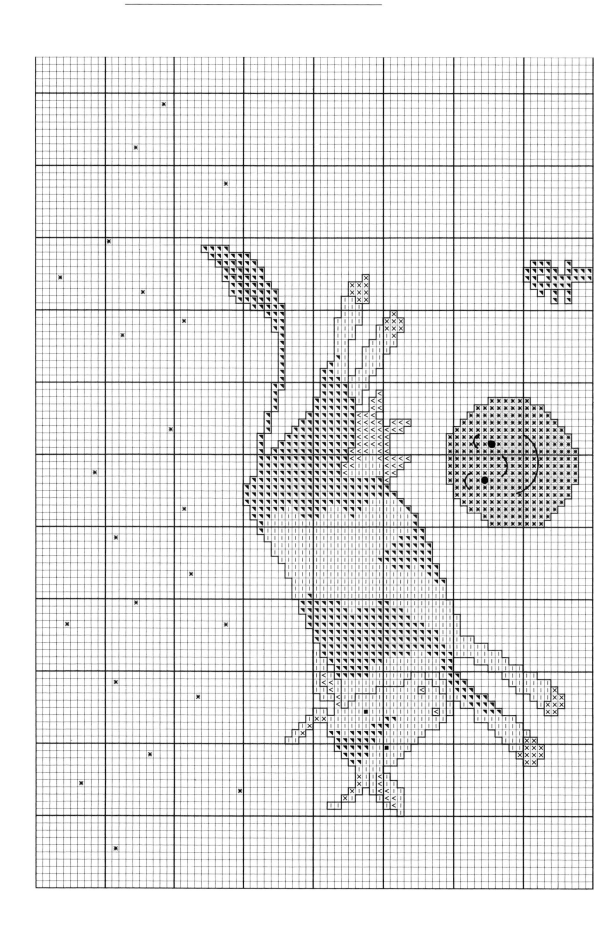

The Cow Jumped Over The Moon

Illustrated on page 35

DESIGN SIZE
37.5 x 29cm (15 x 11½in)

MATERIALS
Paterna yarn, 8yd skein packs:
8 x background colour (552 ice blue)
2 x 221 charcoal; 262 cream; D411 cinnamon
1 x 202 steel grey; 691 dark loden green; 692 loden green; 726 autumn yellow; 934 rusty rose
38 x 36cm (15 x 13½in) piece of DMC 10-count, white interlock canvas

TO STITCH
The original design was worked in tent stitch and finished with backstitch. Use three strands of the thread for the tent stitches and two strands for embroidery. Position the design so that its centre is at the centre of the canvas.

KEY
☒	202 steel grey	⋅	692 loden green
▪	221 charcoal	✳	726 autumn
⊟	262 cream		green
◢	D411 cinnamon	△	934 rusty rose
⊙	691 dark loden		
	yellow		

EMBROIDERY
221 charcoal backstitch for all outlines

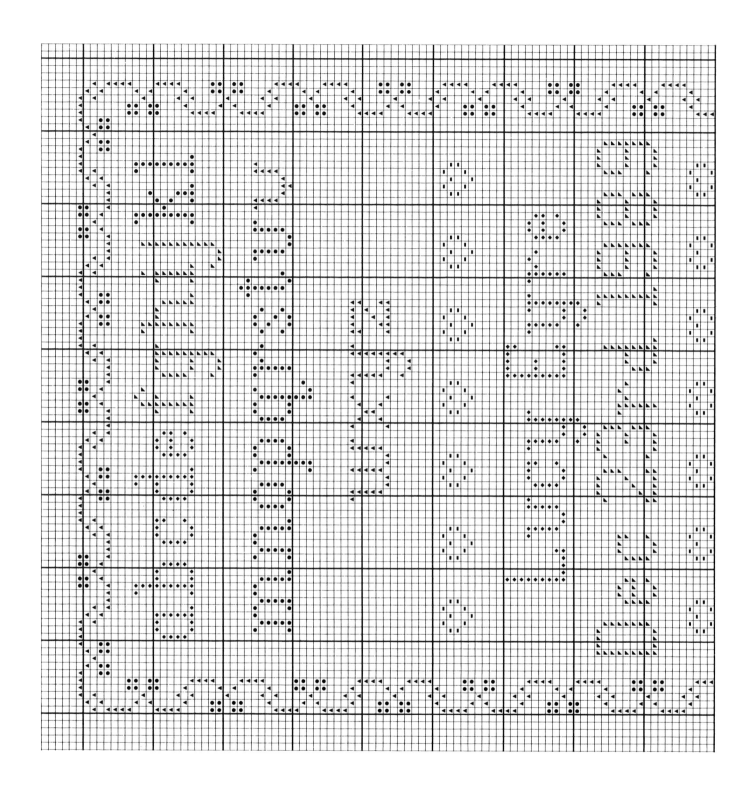

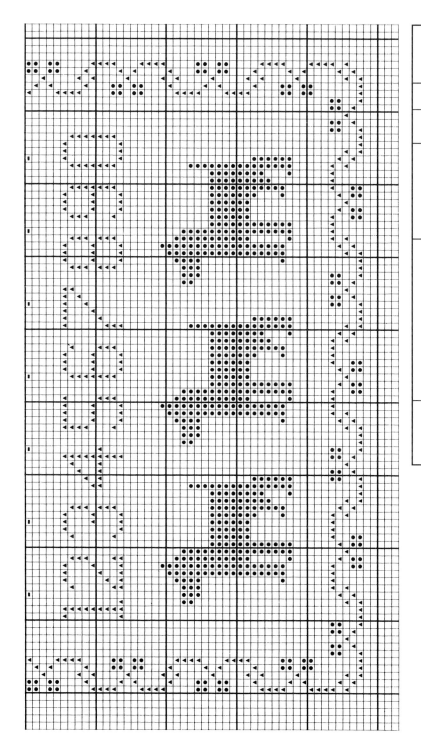

Traditional Sampler

Illustrated on page 36

DESIGN SIZE
18 x 27cm (7 x 10½in)

MATERIALS
Madeira 6-strand cotton embroidery thread, 10m (11yd) spiral packs:
1 x 0402 rust; 0806 mauve grey; 0809 dusky pink; 1703 soft green; 1711 blue
23 x 33cm (9 x 13in) piece of DMC 14-count, natural Rustico fabric

TO STITCH
The original design was worked in cross stitch. Use three strands of the thread throughout. Position the design so that its centre is at the centre of the Aida fabric.

For letters for the child's name, see the alphabet charts on page 114. For the numerals for the date of birth, see the chart on page 115. Work out the arrangements of the letters and numbers on graph paper before stitching.

KEY
⊟ 0402 rust		◆ 0809 dusky pink	
⚫ 0806 mauve grey		▲ 1703 soft green	
		◤ 1711 blue	

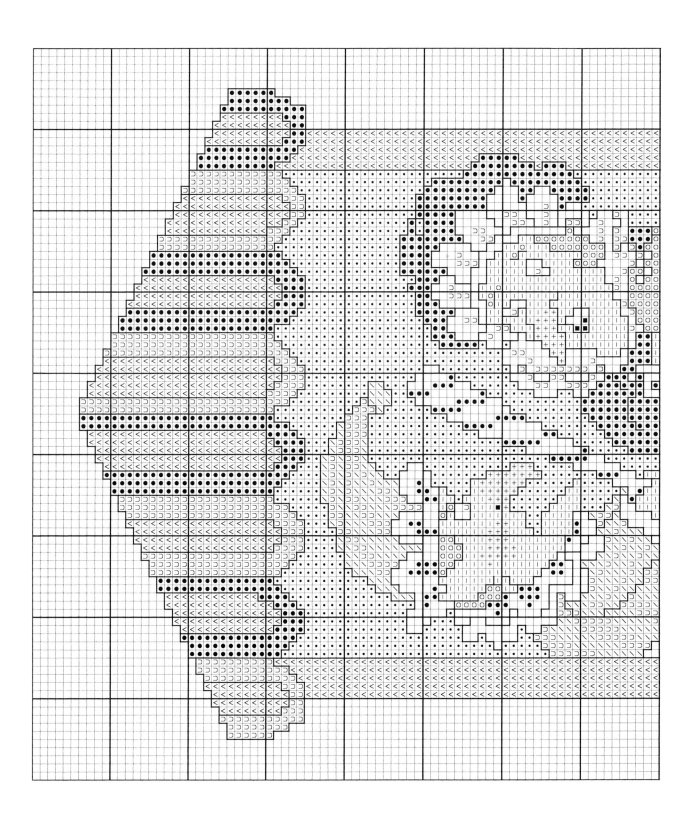

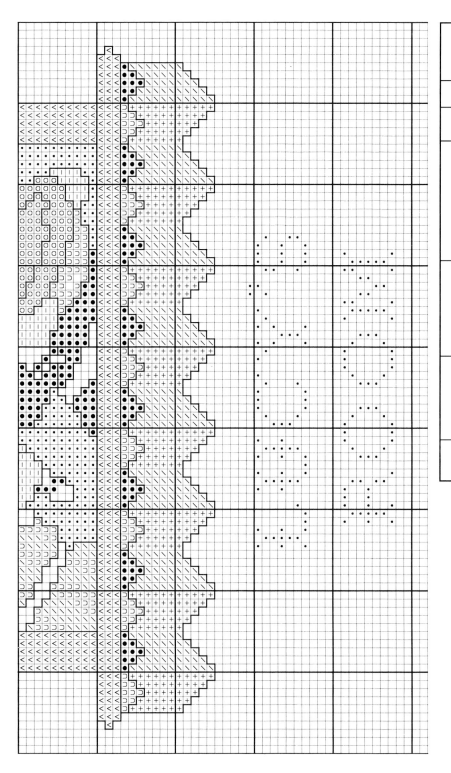

Punch and Judy

Illustrated on page 37

DESIGN SIZE
24 x 16.5cm (9½ x 6½in)

MATERIALS
Paterna yarn, 8yd skein packs:
3 x 262 cream
1 x D117 basil; 221 charcoal; 413 earth
brown; 582 sky blue; 771 sunny yellow;
801 marigold; 875 rust; 951 strawberry;
953 light strawberry
**29 x 21cm (11½ x 8½in) piece of DMC 14-
count, white interlock canvas**

TO STITCH
The original design was worked in tent
stitch and finished with backstitch. Use
two strands of the thread for the tent
stitches and one strand for embroidery.
Position the design so that its centre
is at the centre of the canvas.

KEY

·	D117 basil	⁄	771 sunny yellow
■	221 charcoal	⋀	801 marigold
☐	262 cream	−	875 rust
⊙	413 earth brown	●	951 strawberry
ⓤ	582 sky blue	+	953 light strawberry

EMBROIDERY
221 charcoal backstitch for all outlines

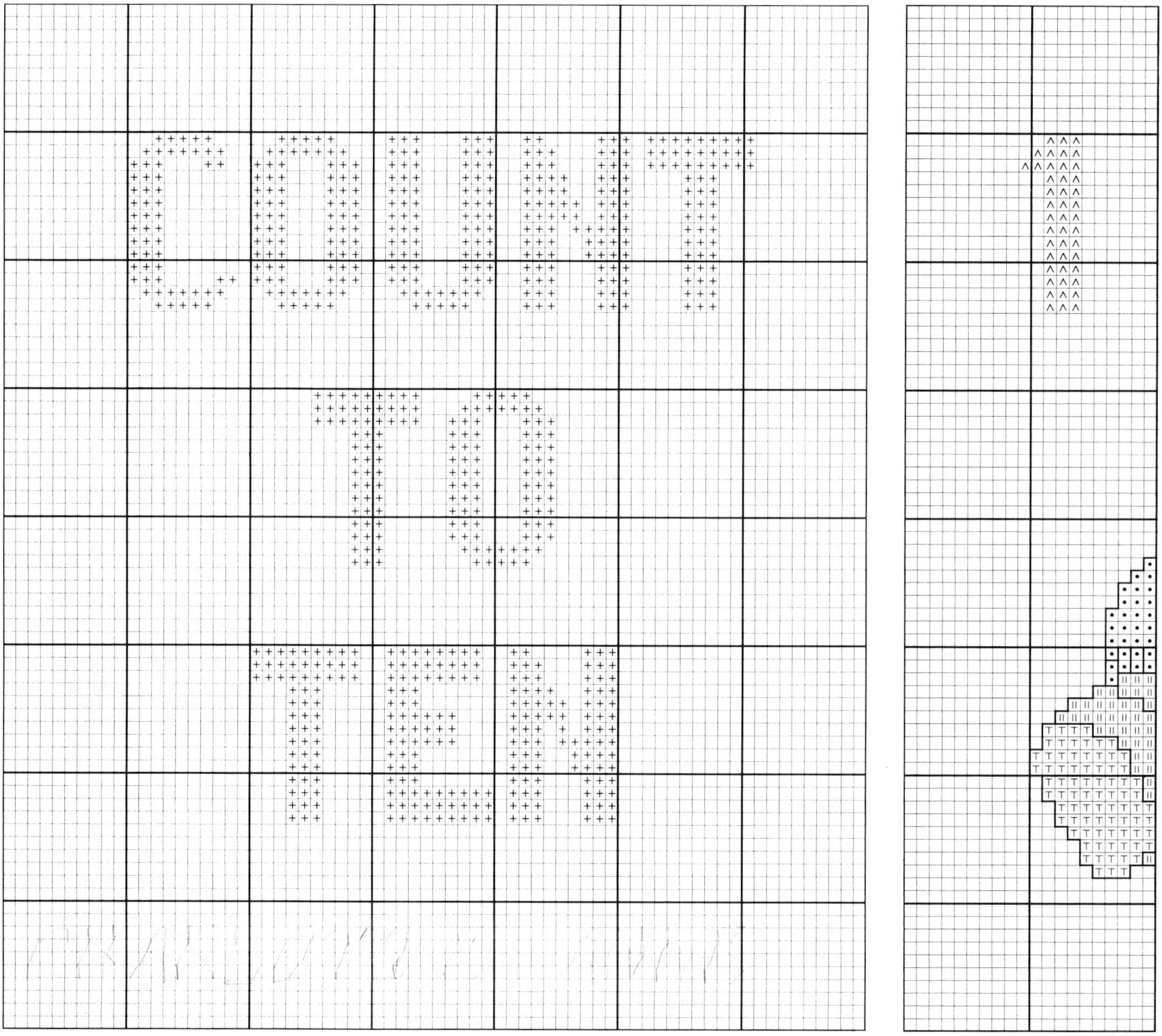

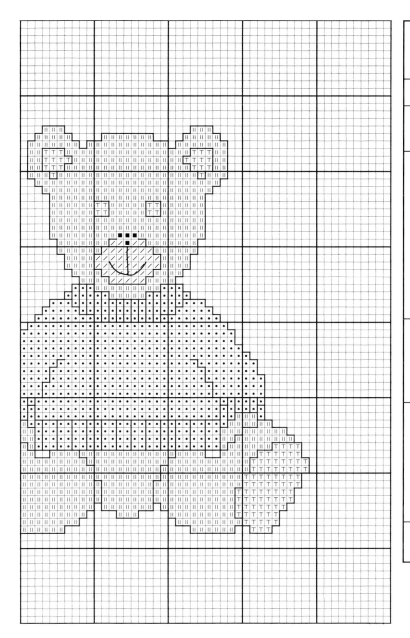

Count to Ten

Illustrated on page 38

DESIGN SIZE
The completed book measures
18 x 20cm (7 x 8in)

MATERIALS
**Madeira 6-strand cotton embroidery
thread, 10m (11yd) spiral packs:**
2 x 0212 red; 0911 blue
1 x white; 0110 yellow; 0113 dark yellow;
0412 light red; 0901 light lilac; 0902 lilac;
0909 light blue; 1211 light green; 1213
green; 1713 charcoal; 1801 grey; 2001 light
tan; 2009 tan
**64 x 64cm (25 x 25in) piece of DMC 14-
count, white Aida fabric**
**86 x 86cm (34 x 34in) piece of white lining
cotton fabric**

TO STITCH
The charts appear on page 98–109. The
original design was worked in cross
stitch and finished with backstitch. Use
three strands of the thread for the cross
stitches and two strands for embroidery.

KEY
○ white		+ 0911 blue	
◪ 0110 yellow		◩ 1211 light green	
☑ 0113 dark yellow		◣ 1213 green	
• 0212 red		■ 1713 charcoal	
◉ 0412 light red		☰ 1801 grey	
▢ 0901 light lilac		‖ 2001 light tan	
☒ 0902 lilac		T 2009 tan	
⊟ 0909 light blue			

EMBROIDERY
1713 charcoal backstitch for all outlines

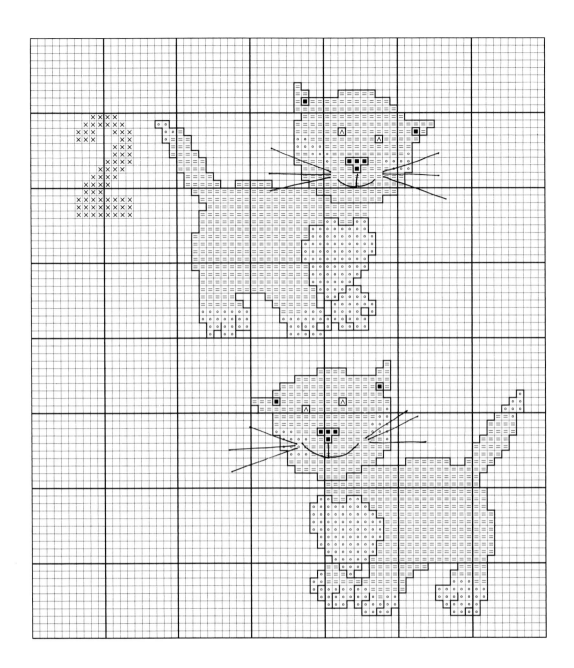

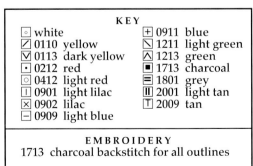

KEY

⊙ white		+ 0911	blue
⊿ 0110	yellow	⊠ 1211	light green
⊻ 0113	dark yellow	∧ 1213	green
• 0212	red	■ 1713	charcoal
⊙ 0412	light red	≡ 1801	grey
I 0901	light lilac	II 2001	light tan
⊠ 0902	lilac	T 2009	tan
⊟ 0909	light blue		

EMBROIDERY
1713 charcoal backstitch for all outlines

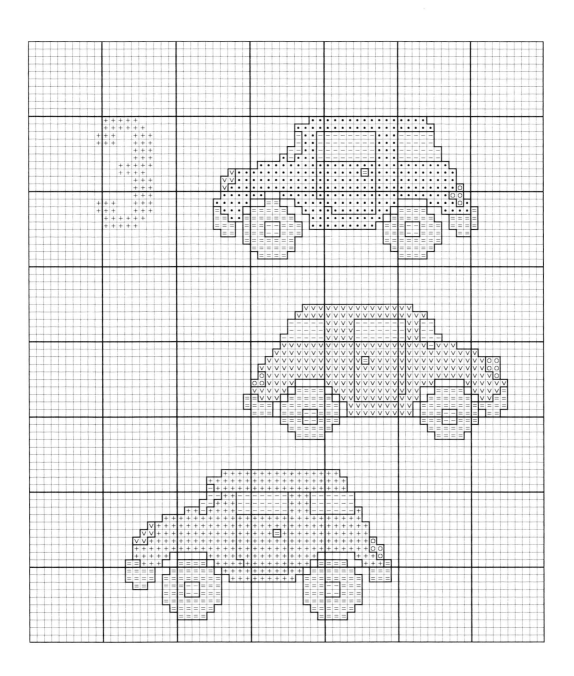

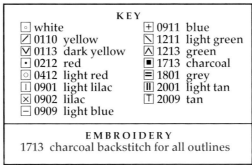

KEY

⊡	white	⊞ 0911	blue
⊘ 0110	yellow	◹ 1211	light green
⊻ 0113	dark yellow	◿ 1213	green
⊡ 0212	red	■ 1713	charcoal
⊙ 0412	light red	≡ 1801	grey
⊓ 0901	light lilac	⫾ 2001	light tan
☒ 0902	lilac	⊤ 2009	tan
⊟ 0909	light blue		

EMBROIDERY
1713 charcoal backstitch for all outlines

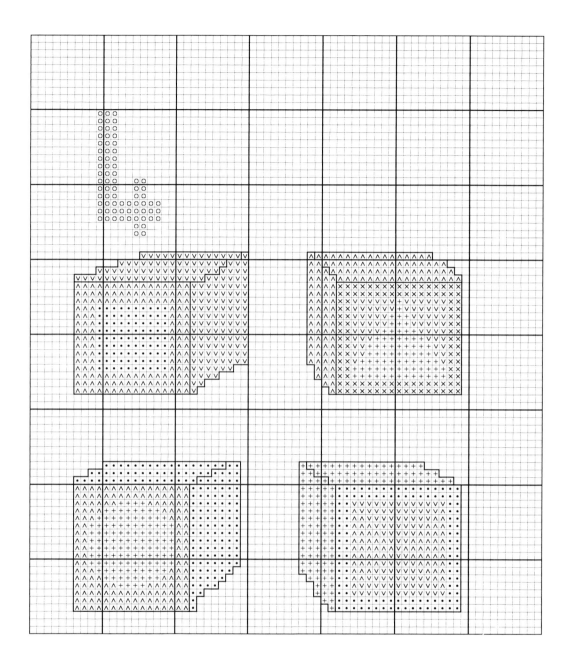

KEY

⊙	white	⊞ 0911	blue
⊘ 0110	yellow	⬂ 1211	light green
⊻ 0113	dark yellow	⋀ 1213	green
• 0212	red	■ 1713	charcoal
⊙ 0412	light red	⊟ 1801	grey
▯ 0901	light lilac	⫿ 2001	light tan
⊠ 0902	lilac	⊤ 2009	tan
⊟ 0909	light blue		

EMBROIDERY
1713 charcoal backstitch for all outlines

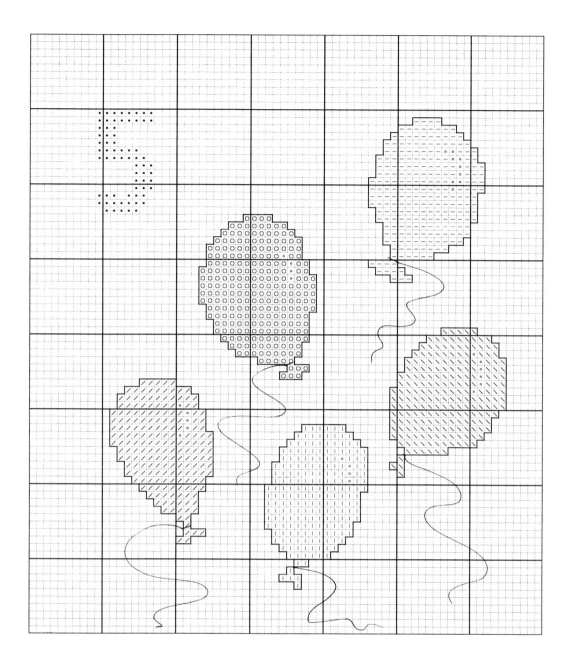

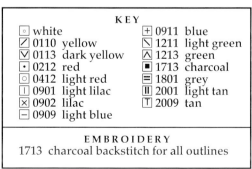

KEY

○	white		＋ 0911	blue
⁄ 0110	yellow		＼ 1211	light green
⋁ 0113	dark yellow		∧ 1213	green
• 0212	red		■ 1713	charcoal
◎ 0412	light red		＝ 1801	grey
Ⅰ 0901	light lilac		‖ 2001	light tan
✕ 0902	lilac		T 2009	tan
＝ 0909	light blue			

EMBROIDERY
1713 charcoal backstitch for all outlines

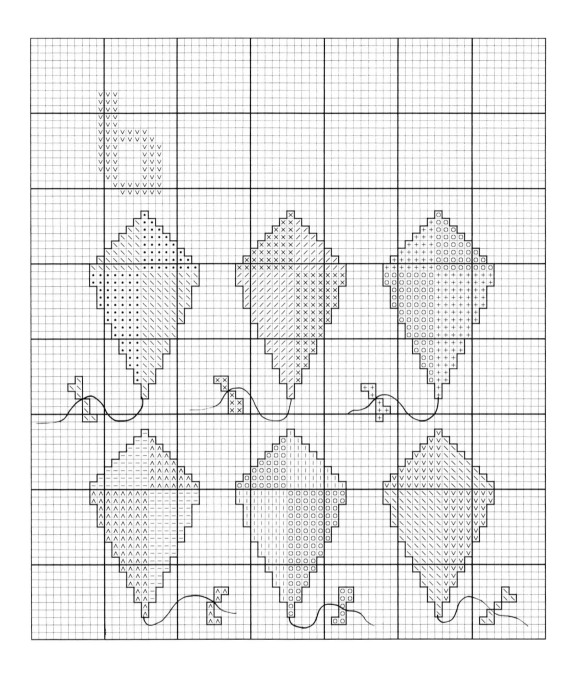

KEY

⊙	white	⊞	0911 blue
⧄	0110 yellow	◹	1211 light green
Ⅴ	0113 dark yellow	◺	1213 green
•	0212 red	■	1713 charcoal
⊙	0412 light red	≡	1801 grey
Ⅰ	0901 light lilac	Ⅱ	2001 light tan
✕	0902 lilac	Ⅱ	2009 tan
⊟	0909 light blue		

EMBROIDERY
1713 charcoal backstitch for all outlines

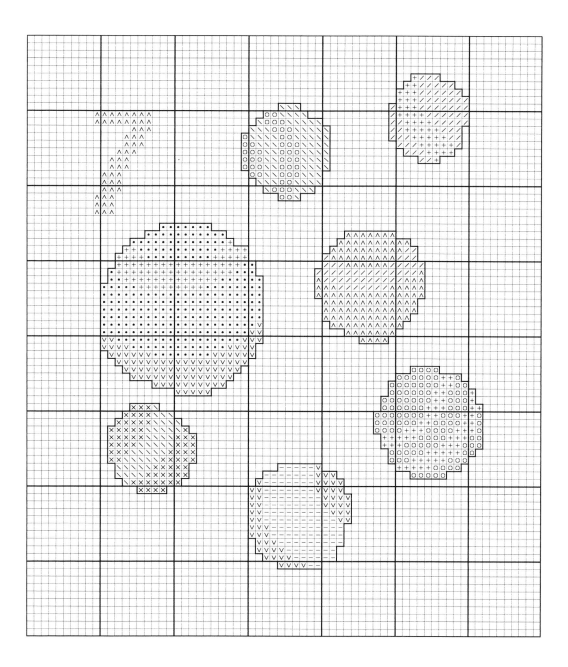

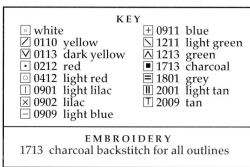

KEY

⊙ white		⊞ 0911 blue	
∕ 0110 yellow		＼ 1211 light green	
☑ 0113 dark yellow		∧ 1213 green	
· 0212 red		■ 1713 charcoal	
⊙ 0412 light red		☰ 1801 grey	
⊓ 0901 light lilac		‖ 2001 light tan	
☒ 0902 lilac		T 2009 tan	
─ 0909 light blue			

EMBROIDERY
1713 charcoal backstitch for all outlines

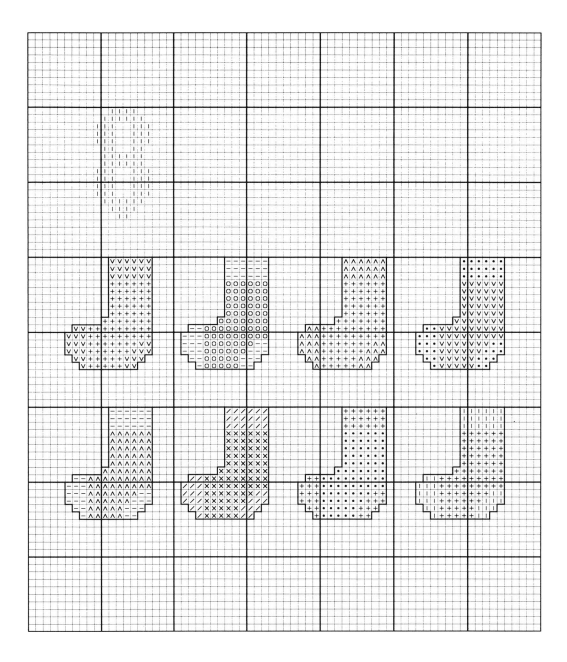

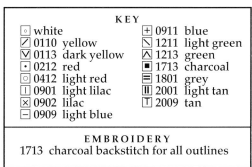

KEY
⊙ white   ⊞ 0911 blue
⧄ 0110 yellow   ◺ 1211 light green
Ⅴ 0113 dark yellow   ⋀ 1213 green
• 0212 red   ■ 1713 charcoal
⊚ 0412 light red   ⊟ 1801 grey
Ⅰ 0901 light lilac   Ⅱ 2001 light tan
✕ 0902 lilac   Ⓣ 2009 tan
⊖ 0909 light blue

EMBROIDERY
1713 charcoal backstitch for all outlines

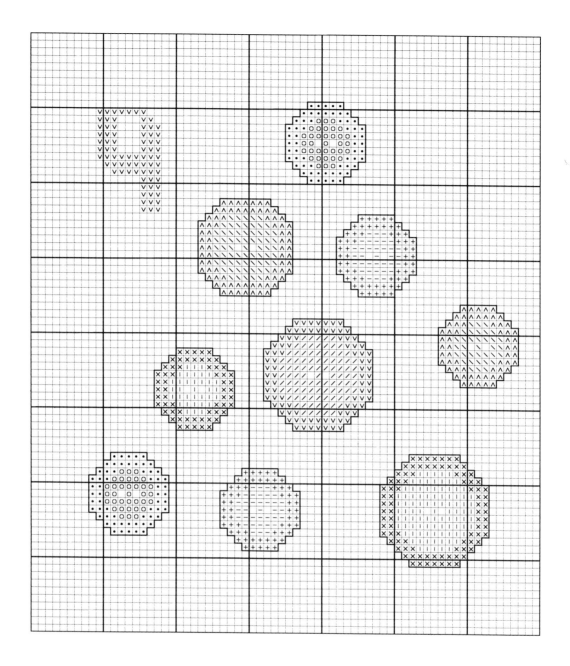

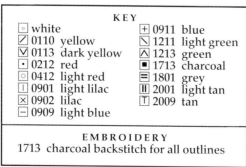

KEY

⊡	white	+	0911 blue
⊘	0110 yellow	◣	1211 light green
⋁	0113 dark yellow	⋀	1213 green
•	0212 red	■	1713 charcoal
⊙	0412 light red	⊟	1801 grey
Ⅱ	0901 light lilac	Ⅲ	2001 light tan
✕	0902 lilac	Ⲧ	2009 tan
⊟	0909 light blue		

EMBROIDERY
1713 charcoal backstitch for all outlines

Panel 1

COUNT
TO
TEN

Panel 2

1

10

Panel 3

9

2

Panel 4

3

8

Panel 5

7

4

Panel 6

5

6

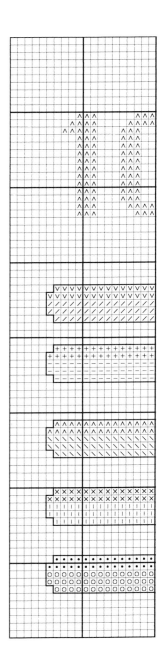

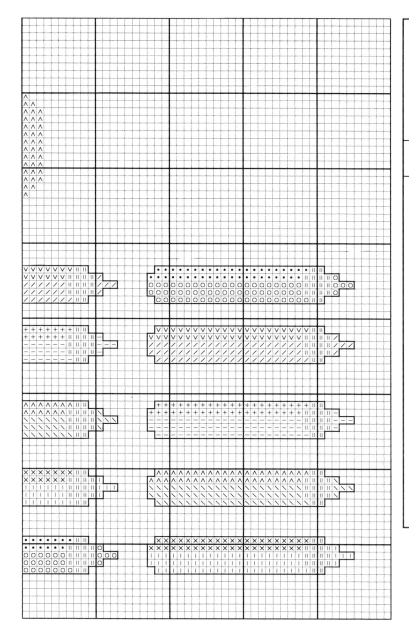

KEY

○	white	⊞ 0911	blue
⊘ 0110	yellow	◩ 1211	light green
⋁ 0113	dark yellow	◩ 1213	green
⊡ 0212	red	■ 1713	charcoal
⊙ 0412	light red	☰ 1801	grey
⊓ 0901	light lilac	⫫ 2001	light tan
⊠ 0902	lilac	⊤ 2009	tan
⊟ 0909	light blue		

EMBROIDERY
1713 charcoal backstitch for all outlines

TO MAKE THE BOOK
1 Cut each embroidery panel to 15 x 17cm (6 x 6¾in) and turn under 1cm (½in) on all the edges.
2 Cut the lining into 6 pieces, each measuring 40 x 22cm (16 x 8¾in). Fold in half along the long edge and mark the centre line with basting stitches. On the right sides of the lining panels, overstitch each embroidery panel in place following the diagram opposite. Ensure that the embroideries are centred to each page. Remove the basting stitches.
3 With right sides together and a 1cm (½in) seam allowance, stitch together the panels in the following order: 1 to 2; 3 to 4; 5 to 6. Leave a small opening on one side for turning through. Trim the seams and corners and turn right sides out. Stitch up the openings by hand. Press thoroughly.
4 Put together the book with the panels one on top of the other so that panel 1 is at the bottom, panel 3 is face down above panel 2, and panel 5 is face down above panel 4, leaving panel 6 at the top. Stitch all three panels together down the centre, fold in half and press.

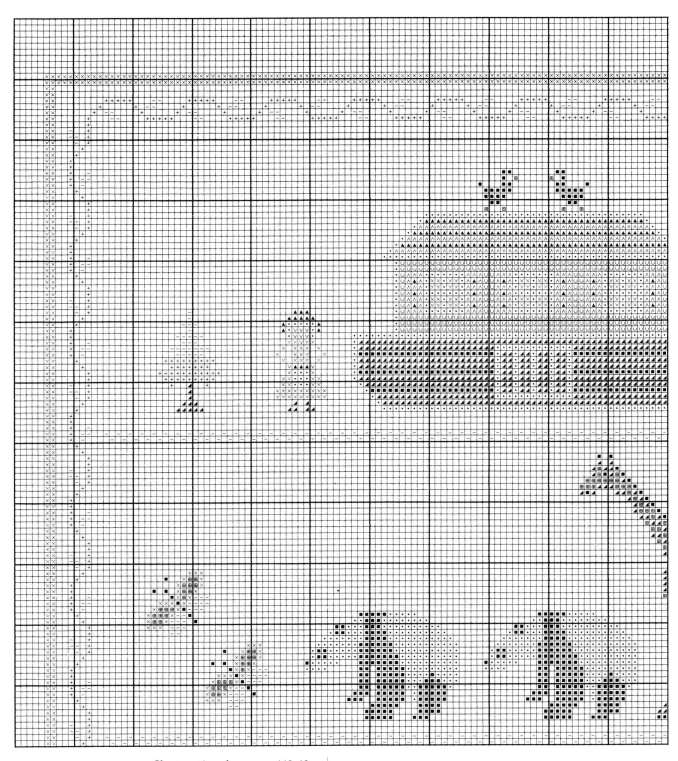

Chart continued on pages 112-13   ↓

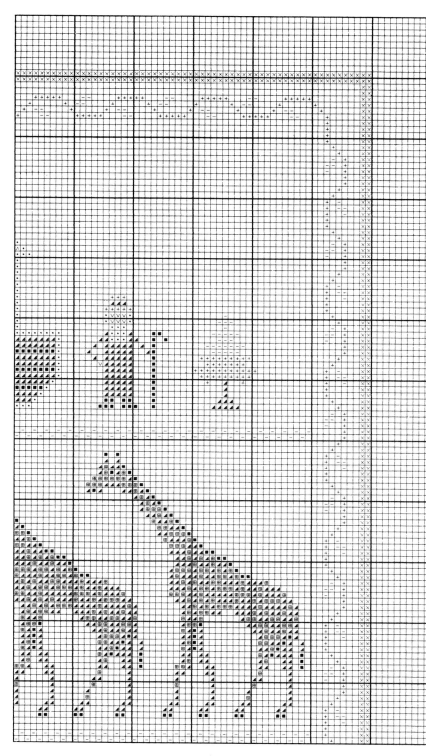

Chart continued on pages on 112-13 ↓

Noah's Ark

Illustrated on page 41

DESIGN SIZE
without fringing 81 x 107cm (32 x 42in)
with fringing 81 x 132cm (32 x 52in)

MATERIALS
Readicut 6-ply pure new wool, 50g balls:
22 x H stone
2 x cream; 17 light green; 23 lavender; 32 camel; 76 nut brown; black
1 x 29 light grey; 31 lemon; 39 dark green; 40 flesh; 50 dark grey; 70 dark brick; 98 light brick
86 x 112cm (34 x 44in) piece of 5-count, cream canvas
For the fringe (optional):
Readicut 6-ply pure new wool, 50g balls:
6 x H stone
Latchet

TO STITCH
The original design was worked in cross stitch. Use the whole thread throughout. Although the rug can be worked well without a needlepoint frame, if you have one that is large enough, use it. Take care not to pull the wool too tight.

Position the design so that its centre is at the centre of the canvas. Work the border and motifs first and then fill in the background starting at the bottom left-hand corner.

KEY

·	cream	+	39 dark green
☐	H stone	▽	40 flesh
⊟	17 light green	●	50 dark grey
✕	23 lavender	▲	70 dark brick
⊙	29 light grey	◢	76 nut brown
⊞	31 lemon	∧	98 light brick
⊍	32 camel	■	black

Chart continued on pages 110-11 ↑

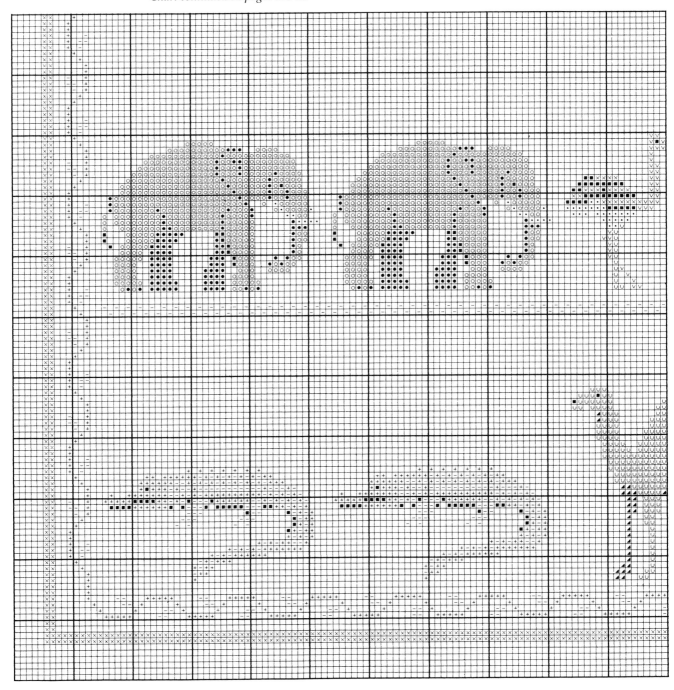

112

↑ *Chart continued on pages 110-11*

KEY

·	cream	± 39	dark green
	H stone	☑ 40	flesh
− 17	light green	● 50	dark grey
⊠ 23	lavender	▲ 70	dark brick
○ 29	light grey	◢ 76	nut brown
⊞ 31	lemon	△ 98	light brick
⊡ 32	camel	■	black

TO MAKE AND FRINGE THE RUG
1 Carefully stretch the canvas back into shape (see page 119). As the canvas and stitching is fairly bulky for this design, the stretching may take a few days.
2 Before adding the fringe, fold the spare canvas at the ends right back to the edge of the stitching. Cut the fringing yarn into equal lengths of 30cm (12in).
3 Using the latchet hook, knot two lengths of yarn into each hole of the last row of the completed rug. Work left to right as follows: hold the latchet hook in your right hand and push it up through the canvas. Hold the fringing wool in your left hand, doubled over to form a loop, with the loop hanging down. Hook the two loops under the hook and pull loop through the canvas 7.5cm (3in). Unhook the latchet and feed the four ends through the loop pulling tightly into a knot. This will form a tassel.
4 When the row is finished, tie the tassels in the following order: starting from the left, take the first and third tassels and tie them together using an overhand knot and tighten the knot 2.5cm (1in) from the end of the rug. Next take the second and fifth, and knot these together in the same way. Continue, knotting the fourth and seventh, the sixth and ninth tassels, and so on until the row has been completed.
5 Trim any uneven ends with a pair of scissors and repeat at the other end of the rug.
6 To finish the rug and prevent the canvas fraying, stitch the selvedge and raw edges of the canvas to the underside.

Sample Alphabets

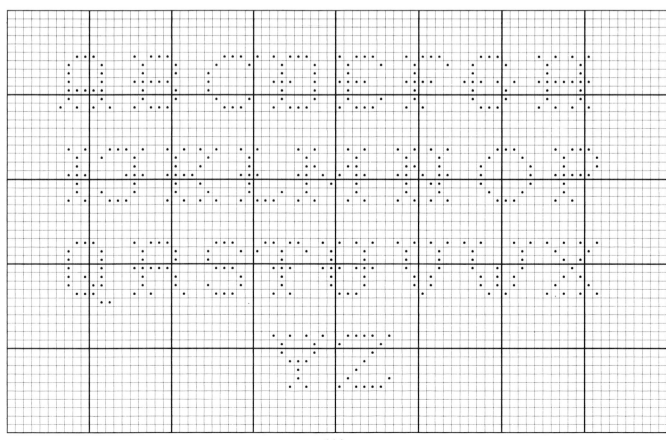

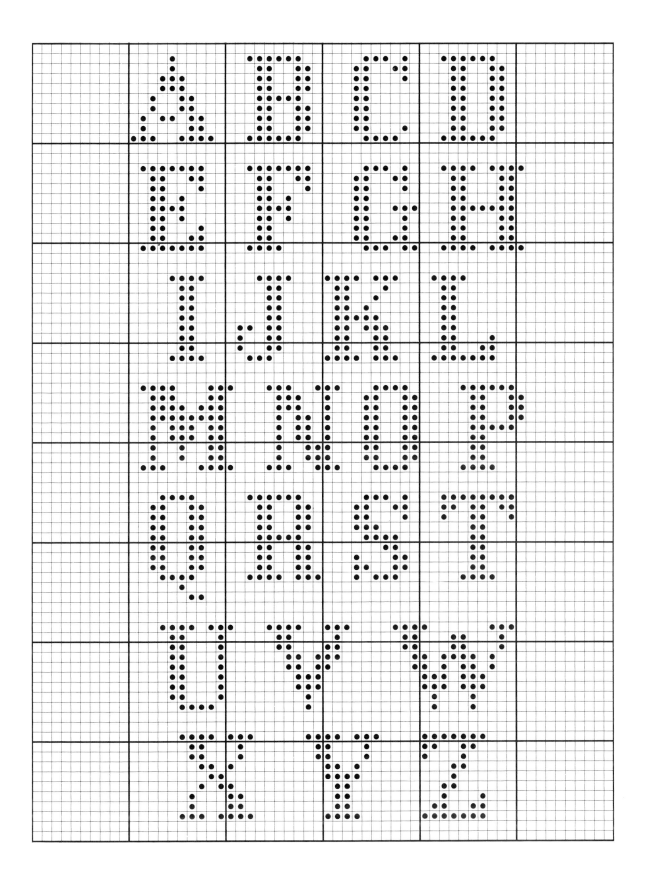

Techniques

CANVAS

Cross-stitch and needlepoint canvasses are produced in various count sizes with specific numbers of holes per 2.5 cm (1 in). In this book, the count referred to is the number of holes per 2.5 cm (1 in), eg in a piece of 14-count Aida fabric, you need to stitch across 14 holes to cover 2.5 cm (1 in). The majority of the designs in this book are worked on 14-count fabric for the cross-stitch pieces, although Lavender's Blue is worked on a finer 18-count fabric and The Queen of Hearts pinny is made from a 25-count linen. The needlepoint designs are worked on 10-count canvas withthe exception of the Noah's Ark rug which is a coarse 5-count.

NEEDLES

Needles for needlepoint and cross-stitch are blunt-ended and large-eyed and come in a range of sizes beginning at 13, for heavy work, and going up to 26 for very fine work. Ensure the needle takes the thickness of yarn easily and it fits through the hole on the canvas without pulling it out of shape. Here is a useful guide:

25-count canvas: size 26
18-count canvas: size 22
14-count canvas: size 20
10-count canvas: size 18
5-count canvas: size 16

PREPARATION

When using Aida fabric, and before doing anything else, cut it to the required size and run a line of hem or zigzag stitch around all sides of the fabric. This will prevent fraying which can cause problems if it should start running into the design area. Wool can often snag on the sharp edges of canvas, so it is worth sticking strips of brown sticky taps around the edges of the trimmed canvas before starting.

Many of the designs in this book require them to be positioned in the centre of the trimmed fabric. To find the centre, the easiest way is to fold the fabric in half horizontally and then vertically. Mark the centre with basting stitches which can then be removed once you have begun the design.

You may prefer to stitch your design using an embroidery or tapestry frame for support. These come in various sizes. For Aida fabric, use the circular types which consist of two circles of wood with a screw across the top. Place one circle underneath the fabric and clamp the other section over the top, tightening the screw until the fabric is taut. For canvas, use the larger rectangular, scroll frames. They help to keep the fabric taut and the tension even. For designs worked using tent stitch, they also help to prevent the canvas from becoming distorted. If you choose to make the Noah's Ark rug featured on page 111, you will need a very sturdy tapestry frame which is at least 90cm (36in) wide. Attach the canvas to the frame as suggested by the manufacturer.

READING THE CHARTS

One square on each graph represents one stitch, whether it is cross stitch or tent stitch. The symbols indicate the different colour yarns and where each colour is to be used.

CROSS STITCH

Work each stitch independently taking care not to twist the yarn or leaving slack loops if using more than one thread at a time. Take care always to work the top stitches in the same direction.

Following the diagram below, work the stitches as follows: bring the needle up through the back of the canvas (1), down through the canvas (2), and up through the hole directly beneath (3). Take the yarn over the existing slanted stitch and down through the canvas (4), finally bringing it up again at (5) ready for the next stitch.

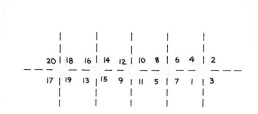

When starting, work the first three or four cross stitches over the tail-end of your yarn to anchor it to the fabric. Avoid using knots to start a new piece of yarn. It is best to make the stitches using two movements and both hands, one beneath the canvas and the other above. This increases the speed at which you can work and improves the regularity of your stitches.

TENT STITCH

Tent stitch is worked as illustrated in the diagram below resulting in a flat, slanted stitch. Working the rows from left to right, bring the needle up through the back of the canvas (1). Then insert it in the hole one row up and one stitch along, ie diagonally (2). Finally, bring the needle back through the canvas via the hole immediately below, ready for the next stitch (3).

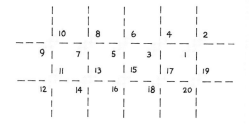

FINISHING OFF

Any of the needlework designs in this book worked in wool on canvas will need to be stretched before being made into the finished item. It is most likely that they will have become distorted during stitching and by blocking the canvas you will achieve a squared piece once more.

Begin by taping a piece of blotting paper with the outline of the canvas drawn onto it to a board. Then place the finished canvas, wrong side up, on top of the paper. If the canvas is badly distorted, gently moisten it before placing on the blotting paper. Gently stretch the canvas to the outline on the blotting paper and pin it securely to the board using upholstery or drawing pins. Start at the four corners and continue along the four sides using one pin every 2.5cm (1in). Use a damp sponge to dampen the work thoroughly on the wrong side and then leave it until it is dry. Once dry, remove it from the board.

Before making up any of the items featured in this book, steam press the embroideries or needlepoints by lying them face down on a thick towel.

AFTERCARE

No matter how much care you take to keep your work clean as you stitch, it will inevitably get grubby. Washing it shouldn't be a problem as long as you use very cool water and a washing agent formulated especially for delicate fabrics. Do not squeeze the finished piece, but leave it to soak for a few minutes before rinsing out thoroughly. Remove excess water by rolling the pieces up in a towel and then gently pull it back into shape and leave it to dry naturally. Always press your stitched piece lightly on the reverse side, lying it face down on a towel.

I would especially like to thank Mum, Dad and my sister Moira Parker for their loving help. Special thanks to Debbie Bliss, Rowan Seymour and David Harris for their moral support, and humour, to help me complete this book.

I would also like to praise the following loyal needlepointers: Meg Basden, Emma Callery, Janice and David Cohen, Rae Fraser, Jan Grice, Ann Hildred, Sheila Hillyard, Elizabeth Hinchcliffe, Eileen Lyon, Marjorie Major, Trudy Smith, and Joan Young.

Many thanks for all the companies and individuals who helped me with the yarns and accessories: Lesley Harmer, Harmer Press Office for Readicut and Paterna Yarns. DMC for the fabrics which I used throughout this book. Linda Parkhouse and Mrs Hood from Madeira Yarns for all the embroidery cottons. Don Cambell from Market Square (Warminster) Ltd for the footstool.

Finally, thanks to Cindy Richards, Emma Callery, Debby Robinson, Shona Wood and Marie Willie for their part in the making of this book.

Address for footstool: Market Square (Warminster) Ltd, 20 Portway, Warminster, Wiltshire BA12 8QD.

*First published in 1994
in Great Britain
by Ebury Press, an imprint of
Random House,
20 Vauxhall Bridge Road,
London SW1V 2SA*

*Text and charts © Fiona McTague 1994
Photographs © Ebury Press 1994*

*British Library
Cataloguing-in-Publication Data*

*A catalogue record for this book is
available from the British Library*

ISBN 0 09 178446 8

*Editor Emma Callery
Photographer Shona Wood
Stylist Marie Willey
Chart artwork Debby Robinson
Illustrator Andrew Farmer
Typeset in Palatino by
Textype Typesetters, Cambridge
Printed and bound in
Singapore by Tien Wah Press*